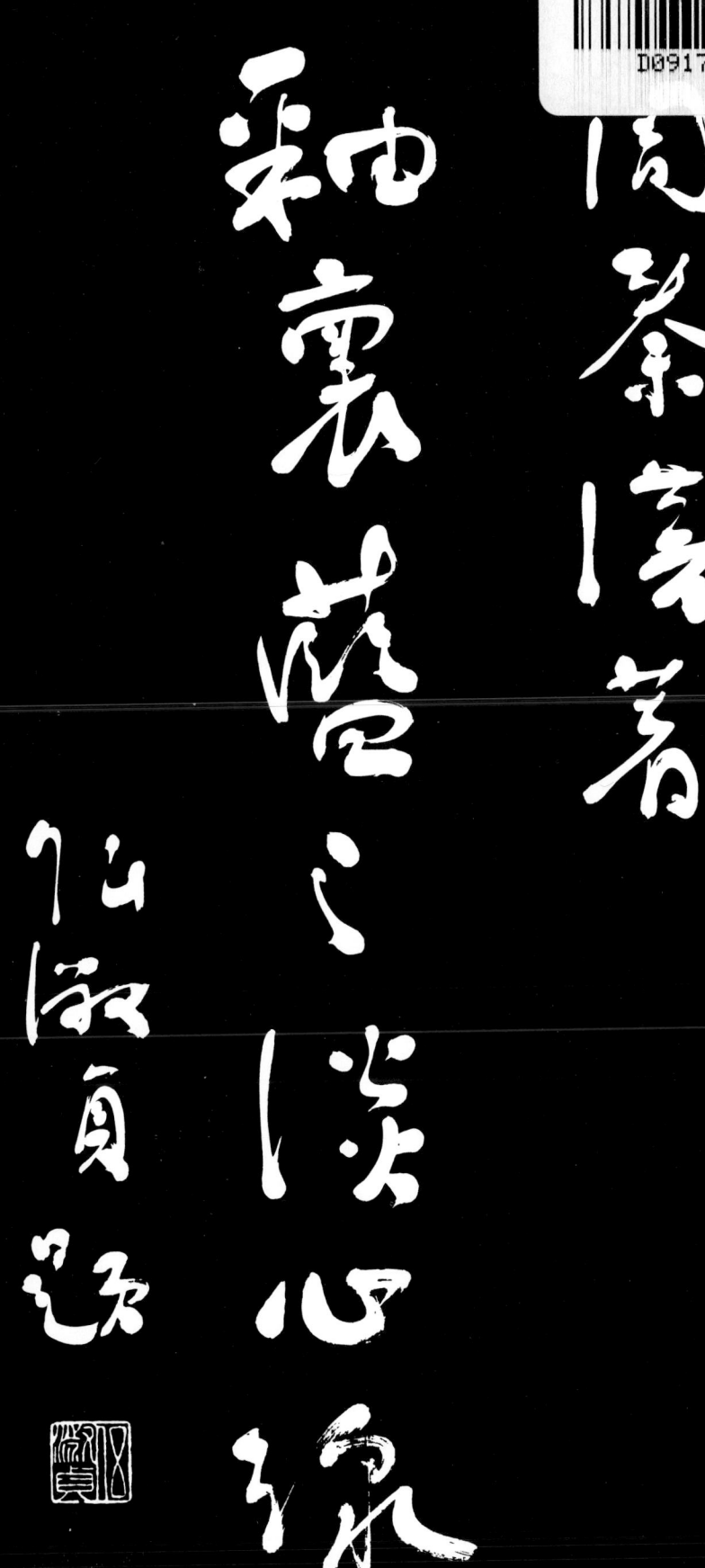

CALVIN CHOU

THE HOLLOW LINE
IN DATING CHINESE PORCELAINS

OCCASIONAL PUBLICATIONS   1978
CHINESE ART APPRAISERS ASSOCIATION   SAN FRANCISCO

THE HOLLOW LINE IN DATING CHINESE PORCELAINS

Cover design, Chinese titles, calligraphy, research and translation of the ancient Chinese texts are by Wu Shu-Chen, President of the Chinese Calligraphy Society, to whom the publisher and author are sincerely and respectfully grateful.

First Edition, 1978

Printed in the United States of America

Published by   Chinese Art Appraisers Association
              625 Post Street, #734
              San Francisco, California 94109

Macro-Photography by Marvin Becker

Figure on Cover: detail from a 19th-century porcelain plaque. A hawker painted in underglaze blue with *hollow line* characteristic (Plates 30-31).

Library of Congress Catalog Card Number 77-87445

ISBN 0-930940-00-8 (Softcover Edition)
     0-930940-03-2 (Hardcover Edition)

To WU SHU-CHEN

*whose moral support, connoisseurship in
Chinese art, scholarly knowledge of
Chinese literature and calligraphy
have made this publication more complete*

TABLE OF CONTENTS

LIST OF ILLUSTRATIONS   PAGE 8

PREFACE   10

THE HOLLOW LINE IN DATING CHINESE PORCELAINS

    Attitudes towards porcelain made after
        the Ch'ien Lung period   13
    A change in attitude   14
    The *hollow line*   17
    Reign marks   20
    Methods of dating   21
    Looking for *hollow lines*   22
    Monochrome porcelains   23
    Twentieth-century porcelains   23
    Special features of the *hollow line*   26
    Grouping porcelains for analysis   29
    Exhibition sales   30
    Collecting trends   30

PROBABLE CAUSE OF THE HOLLOW LINE   33

ILLUSTRATIONS AND DESCRIPTIONS   35

    WINGED DRAGONS

        Fei Yu (Flying Fish Dragon)   75
        "Foliated Dragon" *(Fa Lung)*   77
        Ying Lung (Winged Dragon)   80
        Shan Hai Ching (The Classic of the
            Universe)   80

REFERENCE MATTER

    CH'ING DYNASTY REIGN TITLES   85
    NOTES I   THE HOLLOW LINE   86
    NOTES II   WINGED DRAGONS   90
    BIBLIOGRAPHY   98
    INDEX WITH CHINESE CALLIGRAPHY   102

SPONSORS' INDEX   107
    Publications of the Chinese Art Appraisers Association   120

ILLUSTRATIONS

1	Solid Line	Page	18
2	Solid Line Character		18
3	*Hollow Line*		18
4	*Hollow Line* Character		18
5	Profile: 17th Century		24
6	Profile: 19th Century		24
7	Hollow Line Accumulation		26
8	*Dot* in *Hollow Line*		26
9	*Ring* in *Hollow Line*		26
10	Accumulation in One Character		26
11	*Split Line*		28
12	*Cracked Line*		28
13	Blue and White Incense Burner, Dated 1903		36
14	Pinholes		37
15	"Hsuan T'ung" (1909-12)		38
16	Dragon Head with *Hollow Lines*		39
17	Border Decoration with *Hollow Lines*		40
18	Cloud Design with *Hollow Lines*		41
19	Blue and White Dish, Lotus Design		42
20	Lotus Stem with *Hollow Line* Features		42
21	Bat Wing with *Hollow Line* Features		43
22	Bat		43
23	Bamboo		44
24	Bamboo Leaves		45
25	Dragon		46
26	Claw and Nails		47
27	Eyes		48
28	Horns with "Rings"		48
29	Roof		49
30	Blue and White Plaque		50
31	Hawker		50
32	Blue and White Teapot		51
33	Fisherman		51

34	"Ta" Solid Line Character	52
35	"Ta" *Hollow Line* Character	52
36	"Ch'ing" *Hollow Line* Character	53
37	Kuang Hsu Reign Mark, Solid Lines	54
38	Kuang Hsu Reigh Mark, *Hollow Line* Type	55
39	"Ta" and "Hsu"	56
40	Kuang Hsu Reign Mark, *Hollow Line* Type	57
41	Ming Dynasty Mark, Light Blue	58
42	Ming Dynasty Mark, Dark Blue	59
43	K'ang Hsi Reign Mark	60
44	"Hsi" with *Hollow Lines*	60
45	"Ta" with *Split Line*	61
46	"Nien" with *Hollow Line* Features	61
47	Yung Cheng Reign Mark	62
48	Yung Cheng Reign Mark	63
49	Chia Ch'ing Reign Mark	64
50	Different "Ch'ing" Examples	65
51	"Nien" with *Cracked Lines*	66
52	Wave Pattern	67
53	Mythological Animals	68
54	Wave Pattern	69
55	Wave Pattern	70
56	Head of Horse	71
57	Key-fret Pattern	72
58	Winged Dragon and Mythological Animals	73
59	*Fei Yu*	74
60	Plate with *Fei Yu*	76
61	"Foliated Dragon" *(Fa Lung)*	78
62	*Ying Lung* from the *Shan Hai Ching*	78
63	Platter with *Ying Lung*	79
64	*Fei Yu* from the *Shan Hai Ching*	82
65	Plate with *Fei Yu*	82
66	*K'uei* from the *Shan Hai Ching*	83

PREFACE

A Chinese porcelain of beauty is a joy forever. Its loveliness increases. The memory of it does not fade away. However, to discover a perfectly made porcelain with an early prestigious reign mark should be dated in a nineteenth-century period of "decadence" is, alas, unpleasant for some and unacceptable to others. The desire to associate a finely made object with a classical period is always strong. In the eye of the beholder, the "perfectly beautiful" object cannot be anything else but the real thing, created during a great historical period of art.

The preference for early dating frequently extends to many things that are less than perfect. When an object is subjectively considered to be a genuine creation, it almost never becomes an object of truth. Early dating is sometimes confirmed by appraisers. For some of them, inferior wares are not recognized as products that are made before the nineteenth century. Under these circumstances, late dating is sometimes not considered in evaluating a finely made porcelain that is symmetrically potted, artistically decorated, has an unctuous glaze finish and extremely smooth biscuit.

The Chinese Art Appraisers Association takes pleasure in presenting volume one of this study of ceramic characteristics that probes beyond general appearances. The *hollow line* is one of the more outstanding subjects of discussion resulting from the study of Ch'ing Dynasty porcelain. The terminology and findings come from the research papers of Calvin Chou, prominent collector and professional appraiser specializing in Chinese antiques. This volume is an introduction to a larger and more comprehensive comparison of prototypes and later products in *Dating Chinese Ceramics*. This presentation is not an interpretation of ceramic characteristics but is a record of the observations through many years of Calvin Chou. Illustrated specimens come from museums and private collections in the Far East, United States and Europe.

This scrutiny of details is not intended to diminish the art lover's appreciation and enjoyment of perfection and beauty. The *hollow line* is not proposed here as the sole criterion for dating Chinese porcelains; it is, however, an interesting one to consider. For the connoisseur, porcelains reveal the dates of their execution in more ways than one. For the novice the *hollow line* is easy to recognize and will prove useful as an indicator that certain pieces of porcelain are late nineteenth or early twentieth century and not of earlier dates, as rendered on the basis of personal feeling, popular opinion, or their similarity to illustrations in art books.

The members of the Chinese Art Appraisers Association solicit responses from readers of this publication, whether in agreement or argument. We would greatly appreciate being informed of any piece of porcelain with *hollow lines,* especially pieces with dated inscriptions.

Robert S. Conrich
Chairman, Publications Committee

THE HOLLOW LINE IN DATING CHINESE PORCELAINS

Encouraged by friends to give an exhibition of Ch'ing Dynasty porcelains, I asked Professor John D. La Plante of the Stanford University Museum of Art to advise and assist me in selecting the best K'ang Hsi, Yung Cheng and Ch'ien Lung specimens from my collection.[1] Together with presentable specimens of the Chia Ch'ing and Tao Kuang periods, along with whatever I had of the Hsien Feng, T'ung Chih, Kuang Hsu and Hsuan T'ung reigns, this selection was exhibited in Berkeley in the spring of 1960.[2] In an attempt to show a more complete visual conception of the history of Ch'ing Dynasty porcelain, I felt that the display would be incomplete unless porcelains from every period of the Ch'ing Dynasty were represented.

In 1960 the general attitude among both dealers and collectors seemed to be rather disdainful of anyone who took seriously porcelain after the Ch'ien Lung period, as though either he did not know better, or he did not have a feeling for "the finer things in life." Such an attitude has an interesting background. In 1904 Bushell's idea of the "Modern Period" of porcelain dates "from 1796."[3] Says he: "This is a period of decadence and hardly demands detailed description."[4] In 1915 Hobson dictates that "The reign of Tao Kuang is the last period of which collectors of Chinese ceramics take any account."[5] Hsien Feng (1851-62) porcelains "are not worthy of description."[6] Collectors' interest in Kuang Hsu (1875-1908) porcelain "is of a negative kind. When it is frankly marked he sees and avoids it."[7] In another text, Hobson says: "The chief interest that collectors take in the last two reigns of the Ch'ing Dynasty, that of Kuang Hsu and Hsuan T'ung is to avoid them."[8] In his 1927 book of *Chinese Art* Hobson writes:

> Since the eighteenth century Chinese art has been in full decadence. The best work has been purely imitative, and

the rest is hardly worthy of mention. It is not that the Chinese have lost all their manual dexterity; their craftsmanship is still supreme, as may be learnt to our cost from spurious antiques. But they have ceased to produced anything higher than these. In the days when Chinese art was young and virile it created things which we now recognize to be among the world's masterpieces. [9]

Writing about "The 19th Century" Chinese porcelain in 1945, Cox states that "history now had little effect upon the very sick art of ceramics." [10] By the Tao Kuang period (1821-50), "the wares show a marked degeneration." [11] In 1951 Jenyns entitled one chapter in his book *Later Chinese Porcelain*, "The Period of Decline, 1749 (or 1753) to 1912." [12] Such opinions and widespread indifference could not surpress my curiosity about them.

In the autumn of 1960 I was invited by the Hong Kong Festival of the Arts Council and The Society of Chinese Antiquaries to arrange an exhibition of Chinese ceramics in Hong Kong. I did not hesitate to take that opportunity to suggest including representations from all periods of the Ch'ing Dynasty rather than the more customary display of only K'ang Hsi to Ch'ien Lung porcelains. Despite many negative undertones, the show went on as I suggested. A quarter of the exhibition catalogue was devoted to later Ch'ing porcelain. [13] Up to that time both Oriental and Occidental connoisseurs did not recognize Chia Ch'ing to Hsuan T'ung porcelains as part of any respectable collection of Chinese antiques.

In the intervening years attitudes have changed. Instead of tersely dismissing nineteenth-century porcelain as "very sick art," Van Oort writes:

It is difficult to say whether the high degree of technical perfection during the Ch'ien-lung period gave rise to overdecoration and overdone forms, or whether the decline of artistry in shape and decoration should be seen as a result of the process of social decline which had set in toward the end of the reign. Taking art as a part of the social superstructure the answer must be obvious. However, even if we do not agree with this system of easy reasoning and ready conclusions, a correlation can still be inferred.[14]

In *The Chinese Potter,* Medley says: "not even the disasters of the nineteenth century could wholly destroy" the Chinese potter's skill.[15] He was inevitably compelled:

> ... to submit to the discipline of a factory worker ... Any failures there were, were due rather to the directions to which the potter had to submit than to the character and capability of the potter himself.[16]

In *A Connoisseur's Guide to Chinese Ceramics*, the Beurdeleys state:

> There is a widespread and unjustified prejudice that porcelain after the reign of Ch'ien Lung degenerated beyond recovery. Art historians judge it ... undeserving of the attentions of collectors. Some experts are now in the process of revising this opinion.[17]

As an example of such positive thinking, Van Oort states that the Blue and White bowl with a Tibetan inscription at the Museum of Asiatic Art in Amsterdam "contradicts once and for all the notion of the absolute inferiority of the Tao-Kuang potters."[18] Macintosh points out: "The collector who closes his eyes to the merits of comparatively recent wares is therefore missing a great deal."[19] In the introduction to the Hong Kong exhibition of *Ch'ing Polychrome Porcelain,* the attitude of the Oriental Ceramic Society of Hong Kong concerning late Ch'ing porcelain is that: "Before long (they) should take their rightful place in the long history of Chinese ceramics."[20] In surveying the current trends in collecting, good quality late Ch'ing porcelains with reign marks or dated inscriptions seem to be gaining in importance.

After establishing residence in Hong Kong in 1960, I became a member of the Min Ch'iu Society, a gathering of serious collectors of Chinese antiques. At that time, late Ch'ing porcelain was not a popular subject of conversation. Members' collections included rare bronzes, ceramics, jades and paintings. [21] In the next five years I had the opportunity to see many fine collections of Chinese art. I was also shown countless reproductions in the hands of merchants; studying such pieces is an education in itself. Late Ch'ing Dynasty *min yao* pieces (literally, "people's" or "folk kiln," ordinary kiln products) were still common. But *kuan yao* specimens (literally, "official" or "government kiln," quality kiln products) were already difficult to find. [22] (See Index for Chinese characters).

Of the collections I was able to study in detail, that belonging to Wu Shu-chen, who later became my wife, was the most helpful in my survey of porcelains. [23] Extremely fine Ming and early Ch'ing specimens are a part of her superb collection of Chinese art. When these were compared with late Ch'ing examples of each period from other collections, my thoughts on late Ch'ing characteristics, including the *hollow line,* crystallized in my mind. In my world travels since 1961, I have made my best effort to examine every piece of Chinese porcelain that I could hold in my hands in order to better understand late Ch'ing characteristics and to record the occurrences of *hollow lines.* As I cannot examine everything myself, I hope this presentation will encourage a communication of ideas on this subject. With the respected knowledge of scholars and experts around the world, perhaps they can make the final determination as to the extent to which such characteristics as the *hollow line* can be employed for dating Chinese porcelains.

The *hollow line,* a term I have used for an underglaze blue line with specific features, is a single, short, thin brushstroke with appearance similar to any brushstroke in old or new porcelain. Exclusively found in underglaze blue decorations, all lines seem to be homogeneous in color. However, the *hollow line* is distinctly different from the solid line. Presence of *hollow lines* does not necessarily mean absence of solid lines. Solid lines are expected in all specimens. Whenever specimens of any one time period have all *hollow line* decorations, this does not mean that solid line examples do not exist concurrently. For example, specimens with the Kuang Hsu reign marks (1875-1908) in all *hollow lines* as well as in all solid lines can be found (Plates 34 - 40). The appearance and disappearance of isolated characteristics is not without precedence in porcelain history, of course. Pope's observation of an early fifteenth-century cobalt blue peculiarity is described as:

> ... the occurrence here and there of spots where the supersaturation of cobalt was such that the glaze could not contain it and a black or rusty-brown patch appeared on the surface. These may have been the result of insufficient grinding of the pigment so that small lumps remained, and the technique of preparation must have been perfected over the years for the spots seem largely to have disappeared in Ch'eng-hua times (1465-87).[24]

The underglaze blue *hollow line* does not seem to be the result of a different production process but rather the quality of that process. Notwithstanding the physical or chemical changes in the material, the *hollow line* appears, as far as we know, to be unintented and may be considered an accidental characteristic. A technical analysis of the *hollow line* porcelain and tabulated occurrence of the *hollow line* in specimens from museums and private collections are parts of volume two of this study.

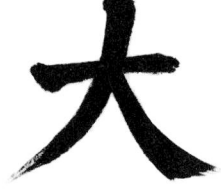

1 Sólid Line

2 Solid Line Character
(See Plate 34)

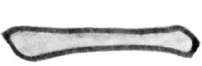

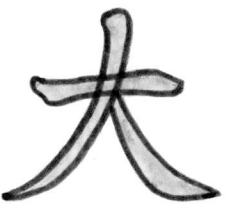

3 *Hollow Line*

4 *Hollow Line* Character
(See Plates 35-36)

To clarify the *hollow line* characteristic consider Figures 1-4. Figure 1 is an example of the general appearance of underglaze blue lines. This is a solid line brushstroke. The whole line is homogeneous in color. Figure 2 is a solid line character. In Figure 3 the single brushstroke consists of two featues: an "outline," and a "wash" of lighter blue color within this "outline." It must be emphasized that the "outline" and the "wash" are *not* separate operations of the brush; only one stroke of the brush is made. Each stroke results not in a solid line but a *hollow* one. Underglaze blue thin lines and Chinese characters, as depicted in Figures 3 and 4, appear with increasing frequency in certain kinds of porcelains. In Ch'ing Dynasty specimens with reign marks, the *hollow line* is seen most frequently in the Kuang Hsu (1875-1908) ones. The appearance of this *hollow line* looks like a diluted cobalt mix. The Chinese term coined by Wu Shu-chen, *"tan hsin hsien,"* ("pale heart line"), appropriately describes the main feature of the *hollow line*. Generally, *hollow line* brushstrokes seem mechanically executed; they look as if the painter was working with "the discipline of a factory worker." Brushstrokes are sometimes uneven, and at other times, skewed. In marks, the calligraphy is executed with a weak hand, and often the characters have poor alignment.

The coincidental appearance of the "outline" and "wash" together in the *hollow line* must be clearly differentiated from the outlining of subjects with many fine lines and then filling in the patterns with graded washes. Many Blue and White export porcelains are painted in this manner. Under ten power or greater magnification, the "outline" of the *hollow line* consists of blue particles along the edges; a watery-blue color can be seen inside this "outline." The minute blue particles along the edge of the "outline" are normal

(Plate 57). This is, however, entirely different from fifteenth-century underglaze blue stipples that can be seen without the aid of a magnifying glass. In some *hollow lines,* the "outline" may be so sharp and well defined that the appearance can be compared to a line drawing by a pen or cutting edge. Although the *hollow line* is not the result of a split brush tip, it does have the appearance of a line made by the splitting tip of a fountain pen. Occasionally the blue "wash" that is within the "outline" may be of a darker tone so it cannot be distinguished from the "outline" at a glance. Detection of the *hollow line,* in such cases, will require a closer look. Initially, the use of a magnifying glass can be helpful in distinguishing the difference between dark solid lines and dark *hollow lines.* The observer should be careful not to misinterpret streaks or faint edges in a solid line and consider that such a line is *hollow.*

As short, thin lines are most likely to be *hollow* such as found in Chinese characters, reign marks become a focus of attention for the search for the *hollow line.* Since a large number of wares do carry an underglaze blue mark, this study includes not only the Blue and White wares, but also three-color, five-color, *t'ou ts'ai, famille-rose* and many monochromes. With reference to marks, Medley writes:

> Any assessment of authenticity must always be based on the materials, form, decoration and its style, and peculiarities associated with the particular type of ceramic wares, and not in the first instance in the mark, which should be considered last in any attempt to evaluate a specimen. [25]

Here the assessment approach is reversed. Inspection of the underglaze blue mark as a first step for indication of age, in this case, is to check on the quality of the cobalt used in writing the mark. Ability to read the Chinese characters of the reign mark is not essential. The presence of the *hollow line* would be but one of the "peculiarities associated with the particular type of ceramic wares."

Discussing reign marks in general only, Hodgson writes:

> It is more than probable that the greater part of the porcelain to be met with in private collections to-day has been made during this dynasty (Ch'ing), even though it bear some earlier mark, for with the Orientals to copy meant that even the smallest detail should be reproduced, and so entirely did they succeed that the connoisseur finds it almost impossible in some cases to distinguish between the two. [26]

Referring to better works of the late Ch'ing periods with "honest" marks, Van Oort says: "Without looking at the marks, one could mistake them for late Ming or K'ang-hsi products." [27] "Were it not for the mark, (these nineteenth-century pieces) would be assigned to former periods." [28] Without looking at the nineteenth-century mark in such a case, an observer may hesitate to say nineteenth century. Yet if the same piece has a seventeenth-century mark, and it is given a nineteenth-century classification based on the mark or decoration having *hollow lines,* objections will no doubt be made. A porcelain having an early reign mark with *hollow lines* needs to be carefully examined. In evaluating such a piece, objectivity is the first requirement. Prior convictions should be considered last.

A knowledge of Chinese porcelain is usually acquired from reading art books, listening to lectures and visiting museums. In such a learning process, the emphasis is inevitably on exemplary pieces. Beginners, and even some appraisers, are only prepared with such a deductive approach to dating Chinese porcelain. Under these circumstances, dating a good quality nineteenth-century porcelain with a K'ang Hsi reign mark as being of the K'ang Hsi period is not uncommon. Collectors who have not seriously considered specimens after the Ch'ien Lung period are sometimes at a disadvantage also. The opinion that a porcelain with a K'ang Hsi reign mark is not of the quality that justifies a K'ang Hsi dating for it may be more subjective than objective. Only with an understanding of late Ch'ing porcelain characteristics can that identification be more objective.

Although the quality of a nineteenth-century specimen may be superior, the ingredients that make up the finished product is not the same as earlier period ones. Ingredients were never scientifically formulated. In fact, no one knew for certain how even the finest wares would turn out until the kilns were opened. Hence, peculiarities, however slight, can be found in the wares of different periods. A distinct underglaze blue *hollow line* is one of such peculiarities seen with increasing frequency in the late Ch'ing Dynasty. Analyzing such details and proceeding from modern specimens to the early ones, in comparison to the traditional recognition of general characteristics and starting from early ceramics and going only as far as Ch'ien Lung porcelains, dating criteria differing from those now taken for granted become inevitable.

Not forgetting the art lover who is unconcerned with such details, one of Hodgson's comments is perhaps appropriate here:

> Having discovered the commercial value of porcelain made for domestic use, and the large demand for antiques, both in their own and in other countries, the Chinese set themselves to work to make and copy these, losing thereby much of the poetic individuality which gives such a unique charm to genuine old examples. [29]

Needless to say, the whole appearance is as important as its parts.

Although *hollow line* reign marks are easier to locate, decorations with the *hollow line* are not difficult to find either. If all lines are solid, then, as is customarily the practice, other dating characteristics must be considered. The best place to look for *hollow lines* in a Blue and White vase suspected of being a late Ch'ing production is in short, thin lines. The entire vase decoration may be composed of a thousand or more brushstrokes, but only short, thin lines may be found to be *hollow*. Frequently seen *hollow line* decorations are faces, eyes, fingers, buildings, key-fret bands, border and wave patterns. Diluted-blue mechanically-drawn lines dominate the features that make up the late Ch'ing *hollow lines*. In some examples, *hollow lines* are conspicuous throughout the whole piece (Plates 52-59).

Thick brushstrokes always show a solid line characteristic. In earlier examples, washes of underglaze blue usually do not have a distinct line at the edge; each layer of wash is an even color throughout (Plate 56). Light blue lines are to be seen in all periods and are all solid and not *hollow*. A light blue line is uniform in color from end to end and is distinctly different from the *hollow line*. Double rings and thin lines encircling mouth and foot rims of bowls, plates and vases have not been seen to be *hollow* except occasionally at the connecting ends of such lines.

If the piece being examined is a monochrome porcelain, for example, a peachbloom beehive-shaped waterpot (also called *"chi chao tsun"* or *"t'ai po tsun"*) recognized as manufactured during the nineteenth century, the underglaze blue K'ang Hsi mark on the base most likely has *hollow lines*. Without examining the mark, such items are recognizable as nineteenth-century copies by such characteristics as heavier potting and more bulky shapes (Figures 5-6).[30]

In early twentieth-century pieces with underglaze blue, the lines of decoration and marks are often discontinuous. Good examples of this can be found in small Blue and White snuff bottles and round boxes for vermillion paste. The line decoration may be of such poor

5 Profile: 17th Century

6 Profile: 19th Century

A study of 19th Century
profiles in forthcoming
Dating Chinese Ceramics

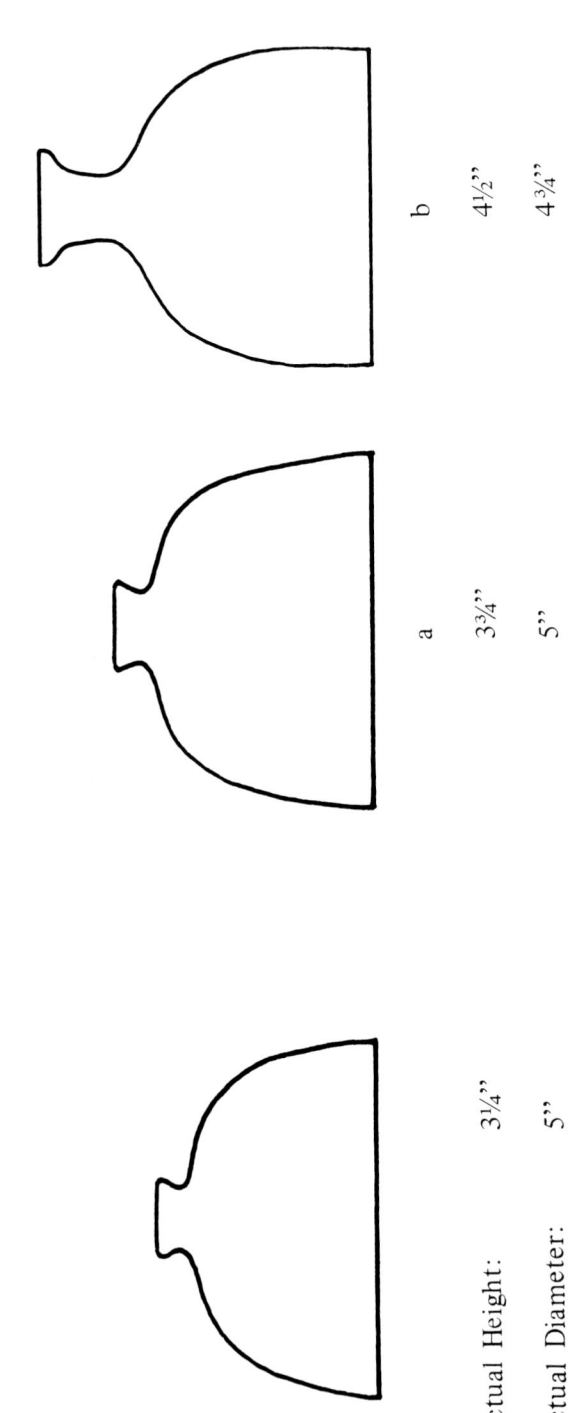

a

b

3¾"

4½"

5"

4¾"

Actual Height: 3¼"

Actual Diameter: 5"

5 Peachbloom Beehive-shaped Waterpot, underglaze blue six-character mark of K'ang Hsi. Author's collection.

6a White Beehive-shaped Waterpot, underglaze blue six-character mark of K'ang Hsi. See plates 43-44. Collection of G.T. Marsh and Company, San Francisco.

6b Oxblood Red Beehive-shaped Waterpot, underglaze blue double ring. Collection of G.T. Marsh and Company, San Francisco.

quality pigment that the whole design looks like a cluster of constructed dotted lines rather than artistically drawn ones. Inferior craftsmanship is common to the products of this period. The observer assessing pieces of porcelain must not, Garner writes:

> . . . be led to assume that because the drawing is inferior the piece is necessarily later. On the other hand, we can often detect a deterioration in style which comes from a lack of the inspiration that governed the original design. [31]

Generally, identifying a twentieth-century specimen is more easy than separating some nineteenth from eighteenth-century and earlier ones.

After the underglaze blue *hollow line* is understood, a reading knowledge of each reign mark of the Ch'ing Dynasty will then be helpful in seeing the differences in materials, form, decoration and style of period pieces. With a recognition of all the reign marks, characteristics of each period can be studied and determined as not being made earlier than the time of the mark. This can aid in distinguishing the subtle differences in certain designs that are repeated, not only in some Ming and earlier Ch'ing periods, but especially in each of the late Ch'ing ones. Garner says:

> The craftsmen who made the pieces and the conditions of manufacture are so different, in the genuine wares and the copies, that it is only a matter of time before they all appear in the right perspective. [32]

With a thorough understanding of details, it will no longer be "an exacting exercise to distinguish the originals from the various vintages of later copies."[33] The observer can readily date pieces of porcelain from a distance, even if the *hollow line* does not exist. Also from a distance, he will be able to pick out pieces that have *hollow lines.*

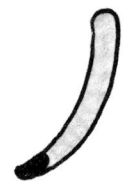

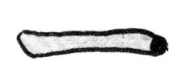

7 *Hollow Line* Accumulation
(Plates 52, 54)

8 *Dot* in *Hollow Line*
(Plates 52, 54)

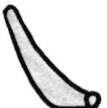

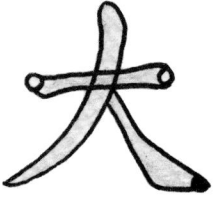

9 *Ring* in *Hollow Line*
(Plate 55)

10 Accumulation in One Character

Fine Chinese porcelains that can be identified from a distance as late nineteenth or early twentieth century are usually the ones that have a more rigid-looking decoration. Brushstrokes tend to look mechanically executed. Difference in quality of craftsmanship is obvious, especially when a prototype is compared side by side with the later product. Early Ch'ing examples are artistically executed; every detail of a design is exactly and neatly finished. Later works may be mechanically drawn, yet brushstrokes are unrestrained and uneven. Early designs are well chosen, impressive and perfect. The later ones are more haphazard and sometimes, amusing. When designs imitate prototypes, then the results look awkward and stiff. The undisciplined hand is severed from the mastership of fine art. At each attempt to revive the old and ideal, only decorative works are produced.

Special features of the *hollow line* are: accumulation of blue pigment at the end of the brushstroke (Figure 7), accumulation of pigment in the form of a *dot* (Figure 8) and an air bubble in the glaze, at the end of a brushstroke, forming a minute *ring* (Figure 9). These are all under a smooth glaze surface. When a *dot* or *ring* is present, it may be at the beginning or at the end, occasionally at both ends, but usually not in every brushstroke of one character (Figure 10). The occurrence of both *hollow* and solid brushstrokes in one character is not unusual. Since accumulation of blue pigment in brushstrokes can also be found in the Ming and earlier Ch'ing specimens, the observer must distinguish the lighter-toned solid line having an accumulation of darker toned blue pigment from the accumulation in a *hollow line.*

Doubtless the observer should also be concerned with the results of firing on the quality of material used. Since the product of unrefined cobalt blue could become a visible blemish on the glaze surface

11 *Split Line*
(Plate 45)

12 *Cracked Line*
(Plate 51)

at any point on the line, the blemish can be felt by the finger. Thickly applied blue may burst through the glaze, leaving a pinhole on the glaze surface over the blue line. If the opening is larger than a pinhole, the cavity is dull and looks dry when compared to the surface glaze (Plates 14-15, 49, 50a). Such frequently seen nineteenth-century characteristics are quite different from the fourteenth and fifteenth-century uneven blue color, black streaks, stipples, patches and the "heaped and piled" characteristic.[34]

Figure 11 is a *split line* and Figure 12, a *cracked line*. Both of these can be considered accidental features and can be seen in the type of porcelains having the *hollow line*. Upon close inspection of these brushstrokes, the blue line is a thin, flat suspension in the glaze. They look like the product of transfer-print decoration badly applied.

Descriptive features comprising the *hollow line* are most frequently seen in late Ch'ing Dynasty porcelains. In order to more clearly define my observations concerning the *hollow line*, I have categorized them into four groups: Group I consists of those examples of porcelain that have reign marks only. Included are specimens dated by inscriptions and documents. The frequency of occurrence of the *hollow line* is greatest in pieces with the Ch'ing Dynasty Kuang Hsu reign mark (1875-1908).[35] Group II consists of porcelains that are generally accepted by connoisseurs as late Ch'ing Dynasty and dated as such by taking into consideration material, form, decoration and style. Group III includes specimens that are presently considered eighteenth century or earlier. Here, consideration has not been given to the *hollow line* in dating Chinese porcelains. Specimens in this group are of fine quality and many carry Ch'eng Hua, K'ang Hsi, Yung Cheng or Ch'ien Lung marks. Group IV is a study of wares made after the Ch'ing Dynasty. Each of these four groups will be studied in detail in the next publication entitled *Dating Chinese Ceramics.*

Late Ch'ing porcelains are now so popular that San Francisco department stores have special sales of them. *Hollow lines* can be found in some of the late nineteenth-century porcelain wares bunched together on tables and shelves. However, most such items are early twentieth century, even though accompanying documents may attest to their antiquity. Inexperienced merchants aggressively sell their wares as "antiques — over 100 years old." They say such dating is based on Far East suppliers' statements. As antiques imported into the United States are not subject to duty, duty-free entry of such merchandise is considered to be official recognition of the suppliers' statements. However, included in such shipments are Blue and White incense burners, some are about eight inches in height and ten inches in diameter and have a cartouche between two dragons (Plate 13). If it were not for the underglaze blue dated inscriptions on them, translated as the "twenty-second year of Kuang Hsu" (in 1896) or the "tenth year of the Republic of China" (in 1921), the knowledgeable onlooker would receive unwelcoming treatment from salespeople for making comments that are contrary to what they have been told to be officially certified, genuine antiques.[36]

With changes in attitude and greater acceptance of late Ch'ing porcelain among collectors around the world, to see Kuang Hsu and Hsuan T'ung marked Blue and White porcelains selling in a local auction house at four to five hundred dollars each is not surprising.[37] In the 1960 Western retail market, such objects were available for less than fifty dollars each. Today, in the Orient, wholesale prices are even higher than such auction prices. In the 1960 Hong Kong antique market, lotus-design Blue and White plates with the T'ung Chih or Kuang Hsu marks that could be easily found for less than five American dollars are now priced at one hundred fifty or more.[38] In addition, not only is the price higher today, but the quality, lower. As older porcelain supplies are exhausted from Far East markets, their current prices seem to reflect an unrealistic valuation of the left-overs. Such remainders among modern wares too easily become "precious" objects. At the same San Francisco auction mentioned above, other Blue and White pieces with Ch'ien Lung dates or marks did not seem to me to warrant the one to three-thousand-dollar bids given to them.[39] In order to help restrain excessive bids for such late pieces bearing early period marks, perhaps a *hollow line* or two can be found. Let us all take another look.

As we find more and more K'ang Hsi pieces with late Ch'ing characteristics, we must realize that genuine K'ang Hsi specimens are relatively uncommon and are thus deserving of additional premiums. Good quality late Ch'ing specimens, because of their increasing scarcity, should appreciate steadily in value. At Far Eastern sources even less-than-perfect nineteenth-century porcelains are now priced well above the prices for similar but perfect pieces in the United States. This condition can only give increasingly more substantial values to late Ch'ing Dynasty porcelains in the Western world.[40]   In addition, as Hsuan T'ung (1909 - 12) porcelains become "art property," export restrictions will be imposed on them in China.

PROBABLE CAUSE OF THE HOLLOW LINE

A technical analysis of the *hollow line* characteristic is to be included in the forthcoming *Dating Chinese Ceramics*. The following is a preliminary comment by Professor John D. La Plante of Stanford University:

> It seems to me that the basic cause of the *hollow line* must be the thinness of the cobalt mix. It may lack a binder used in earlier periods. We know that both oil and glues were used to facilitate the application of the underglaze blue as well as overglaze enamels. In my view, the *hollow line* must result from minimal use of binder. Perhaps only water was used to mix with the ground cobalt, or perhaps just an insufficient amount of binder, resulting in an inability of the mix to hold the ground mineral in suspension thick enough to make an even blue line. The watery mix allowed the particles to move around whereas the thicker binder would hold them - as the liquid was absorbed the particles would move toward the edges and ends of the stroke - where the brush hesitated at beginning or end of strokes or at changes of directions, the deposited layer would be thicker and therefore darker.
>
> Basically the effect is the same as a "water mark" in a water-color wash where the particles of mineral tend to flock to the outer edges of the blemish due to too much water (or at least to more water than the surrounding areas) making it dry at a different rate. The hard edges of such blemishes are caused by mineral particles without binder floating toward the periphery in the manner of the *hollow line.*

The above comment comes from a private communication between Professor La Plante and the author. It is quoted here with the permission of both persons.   R. S. C.

PHOTOGRAPHIC ILLUSTRATIONS

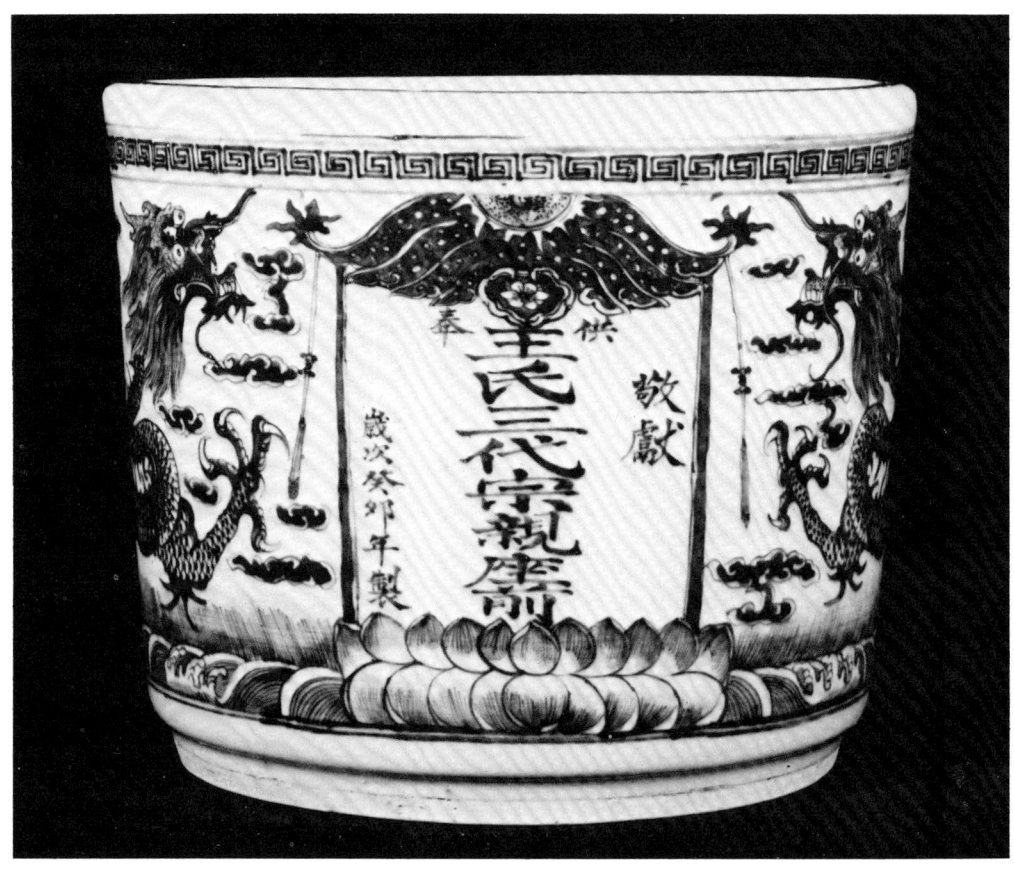

13   Blue and White Incense Burner, Dated 1903.
      Description of this specimen from a July 15, 1977 appraisal report is-
      sued by Chou Ch'in Han & Associates of San Francisco:

> A historically significant porcelain incense burner, painted
> in underglaze blue, straight-sided, wide cylindrical form,
> on ring foot, unglazed base and well bottom. Between two
> dragons, a cartouche containing an eighteen-character in-
> scription indicating that this is an altar piece dedicated to
> three generations of the Wang family and dated in the cy-
> clical year of "kuei mao." On the basis of materials, style of
> decoration and provenance, the Chinese cyclical year cor-
> responds to the year 1903. On the other side and near the
> rim, a four-character inscription: "Tai Tung kou ching"
> ("I, Tai Tung, donate this with deepest respect").
>
> Height: 8½ inches.   Diameter: 10½ inches.

Collected by Mr. and Mrs. Morton G. Baruh, San Francisco, as a dated
specimen of the late Ch'ing Dynasty. Significant for the study of dating
Chinese porcelain, this incense burner was purchased from an exhibition sale in San Francisco in 1977. See Notes I, no. 36. To a collector

this piece may have all the obvious characteristics of the Kuang Hsu period. For a novice unable to read the cyclical year mark without a reign title, he would be unable to tell this piece was made in 1903. Unaware of a previous identification, a person may even translate such a cyclical year mark as 1843. Hopefully, he will not think of an earlier date, nor 1963, based on characteristics of the piece that should be understood to be of the Kuang Hsu period (1875 - 1908).

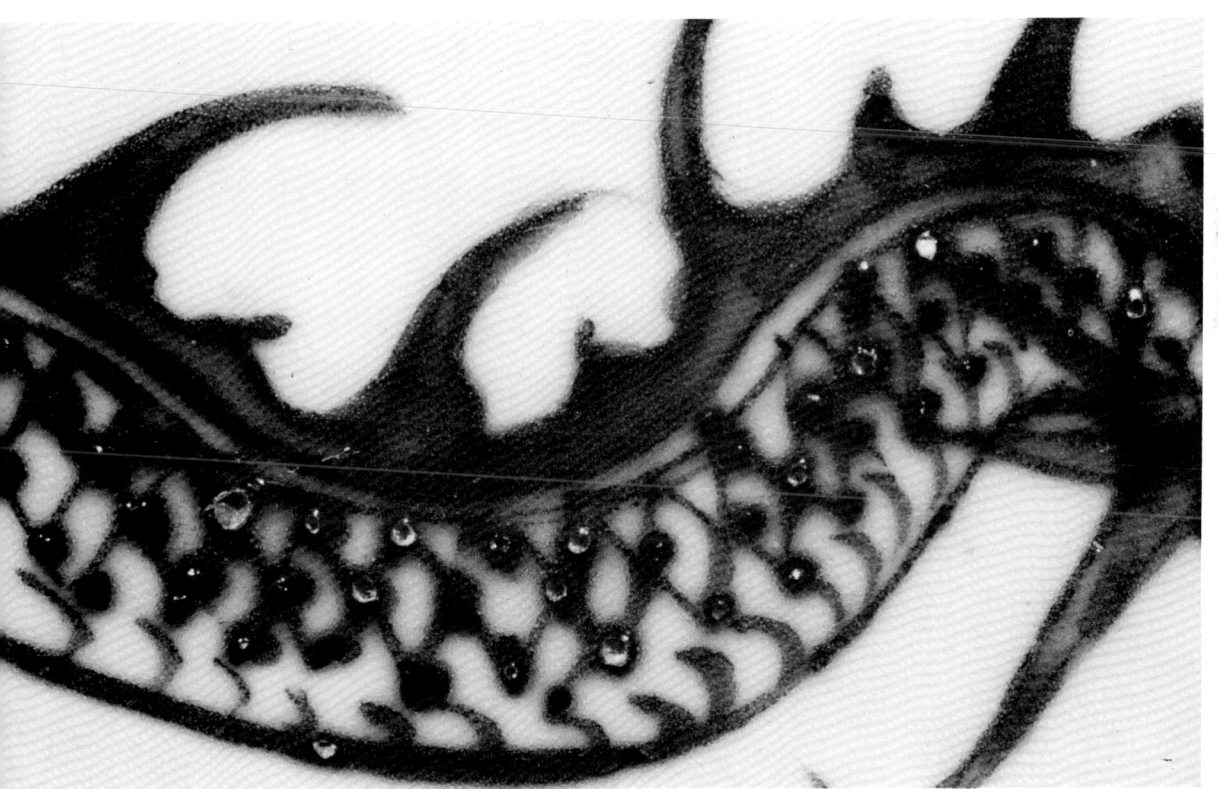

14   Detail. Tail end of dragon, in 1903 incense burner in Plate 13. Pinholes in the glaze. Thick cobalt blue bursting through glaze surface, exposing biscuit below. Seen in many late Ch'ing specimens, pitting can be felt with fingers. See similar pinholes and glaze blemish in Plates 15, 39-40, 49-50a.

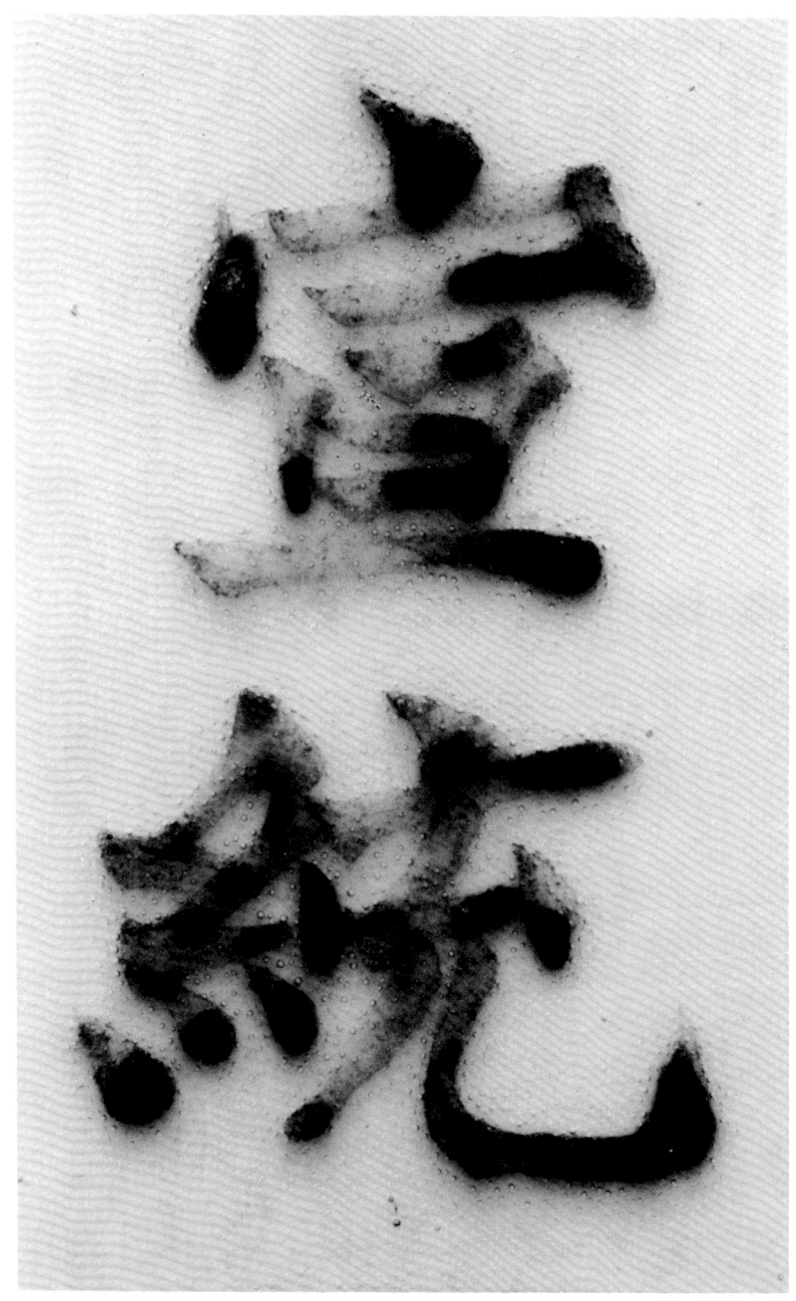

15 Detail. "Hsuan T'ung," reign title of the last period of the
Ch'ing Dynasty (1909 - 12). *Hollow line* type, with accumulations at ends of brushstrokes (see pages 26 - 27), with
punctured glaze surface on character "Hsuan." From a Blue
and White specimen. Actual size of two characters is one
inch in height. Private collection.

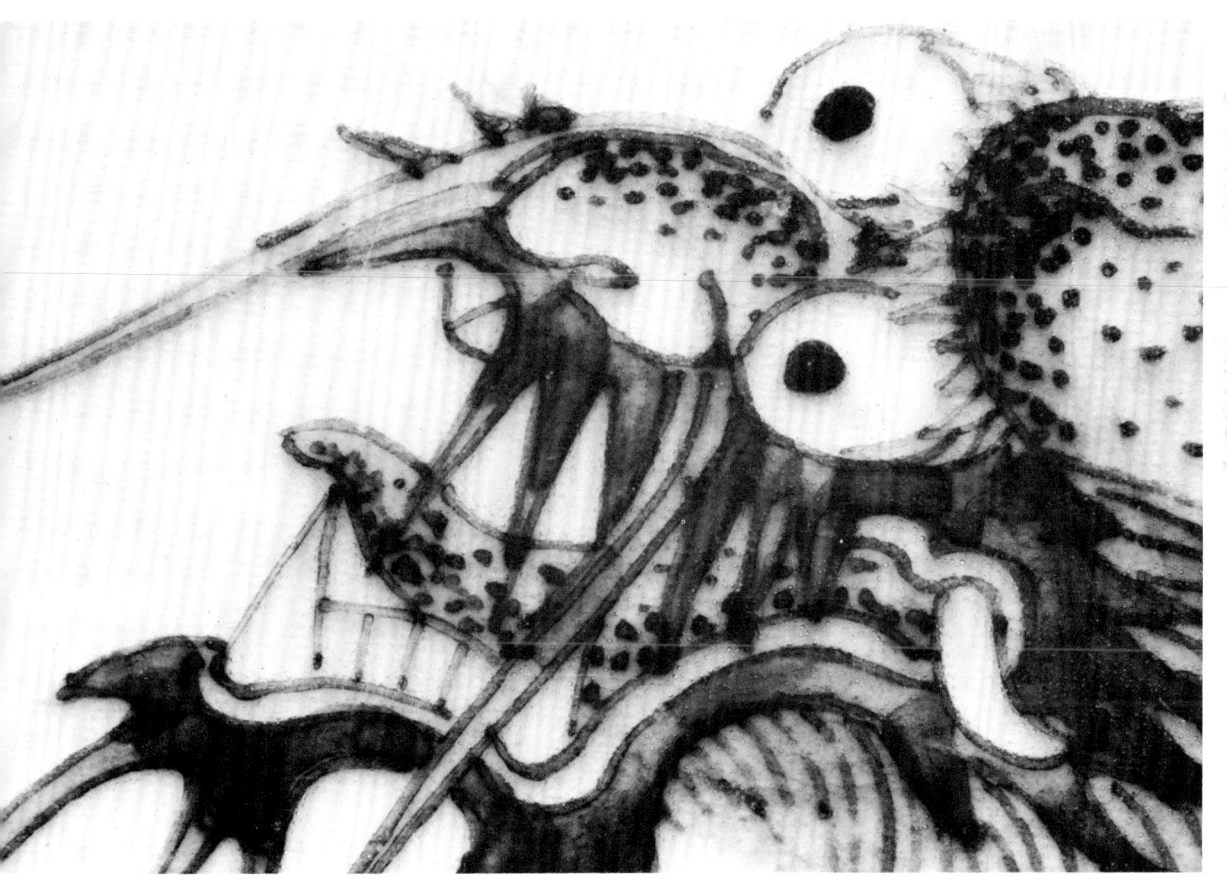

16   Detail. Dragon head, whiskers and teeth with conspicuous *hollow lines.* From specimen in Plate 15. Actual size of area: 1¼" high, 1½" wide.

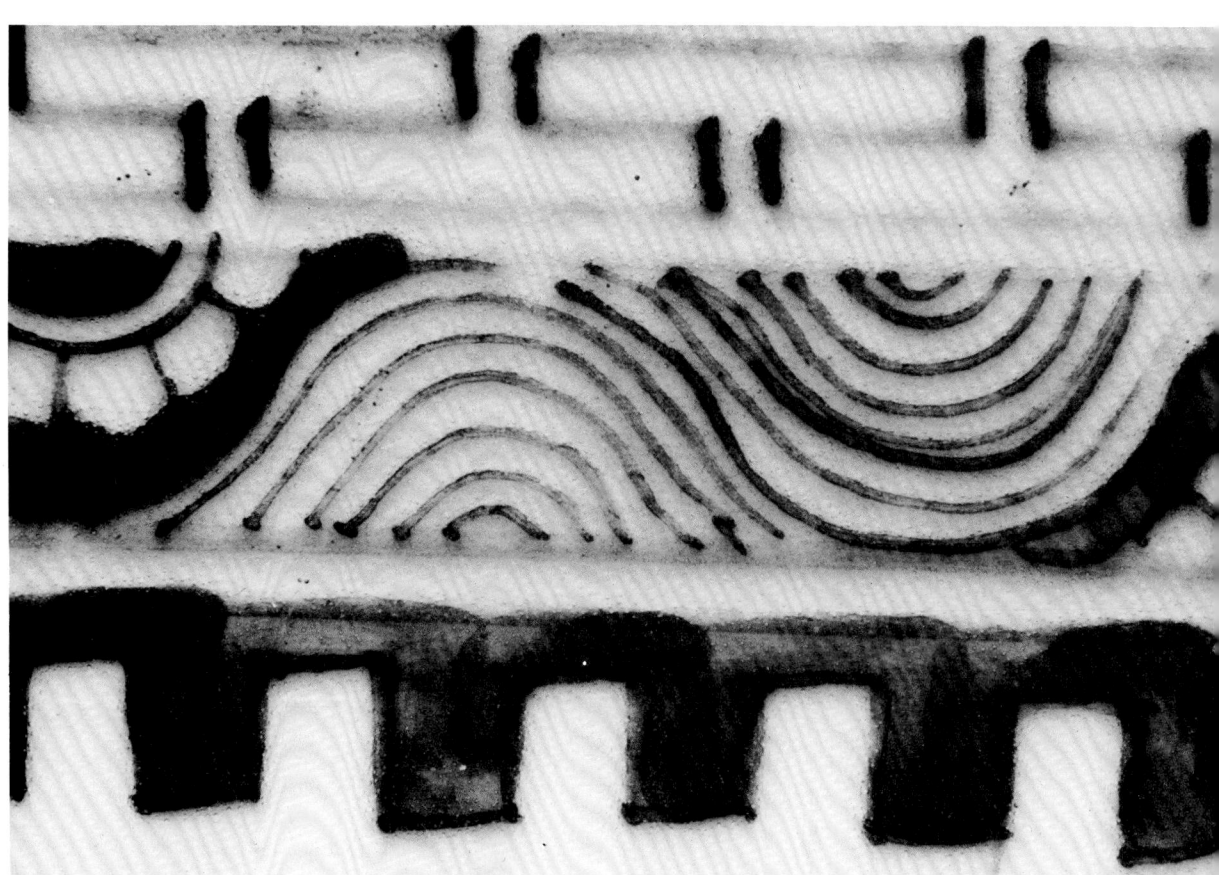

17　Detail. Border decoration, wave band with *hollow lines.* Inconsistent color quality of line decoration is often seen in late Ch'ing wares. Unevenly drawn lines, one running into another, are common also. From specimen in Plates 15-16.

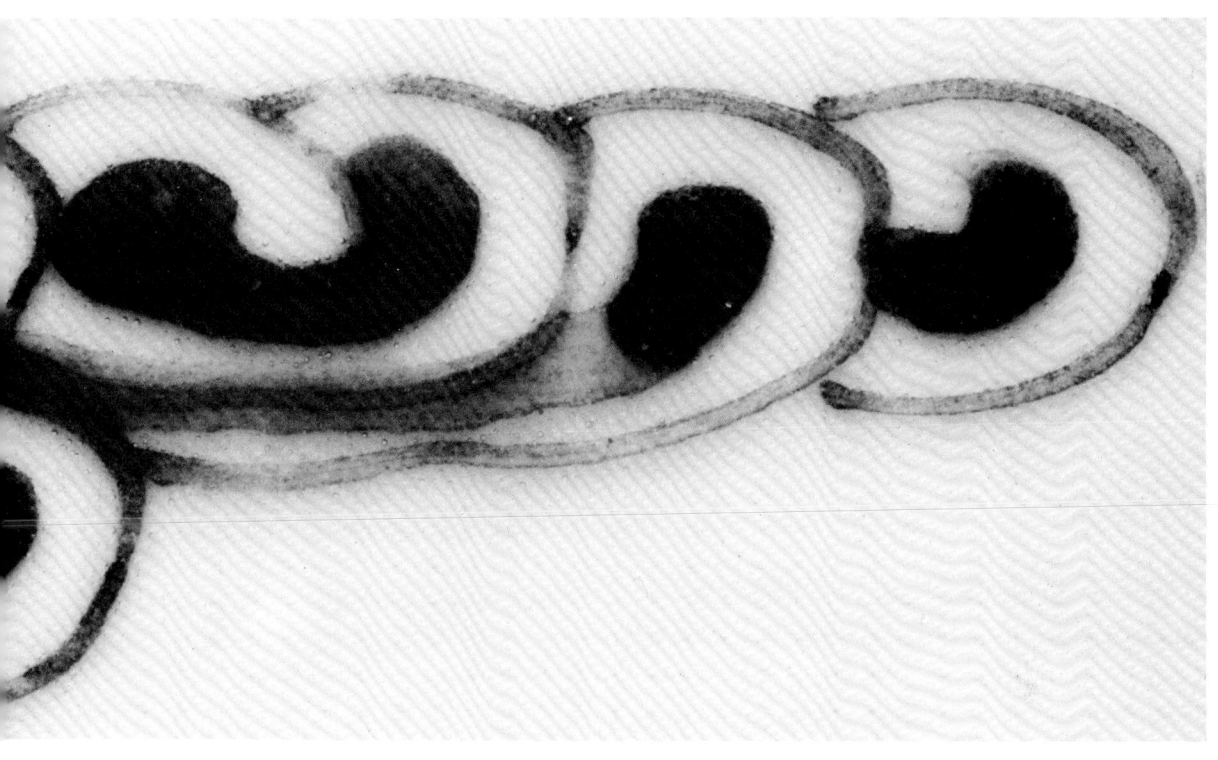

18

18 Detail. Cloud design, with *hollow lines.* From specimen in Plates 15-17. Illustrations of entire specimens and their details in forthcoming book *Dating Chinese Ceramics.*

19 Blue and White Dish, lotus design, six-character mark of Kuang Hsu (1875-1908). 1½" H., 6" D. See Notes I, no. 38. Private collection.

20 Detail. Lotus stem with *hollow line* features. Flower and stem: 1" H. From dish in Plate 19.

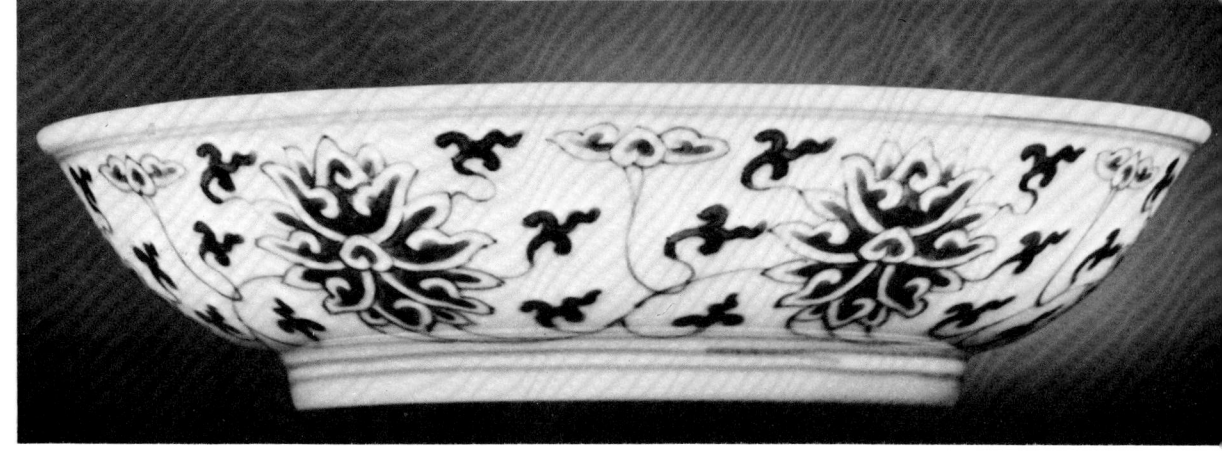

19

20

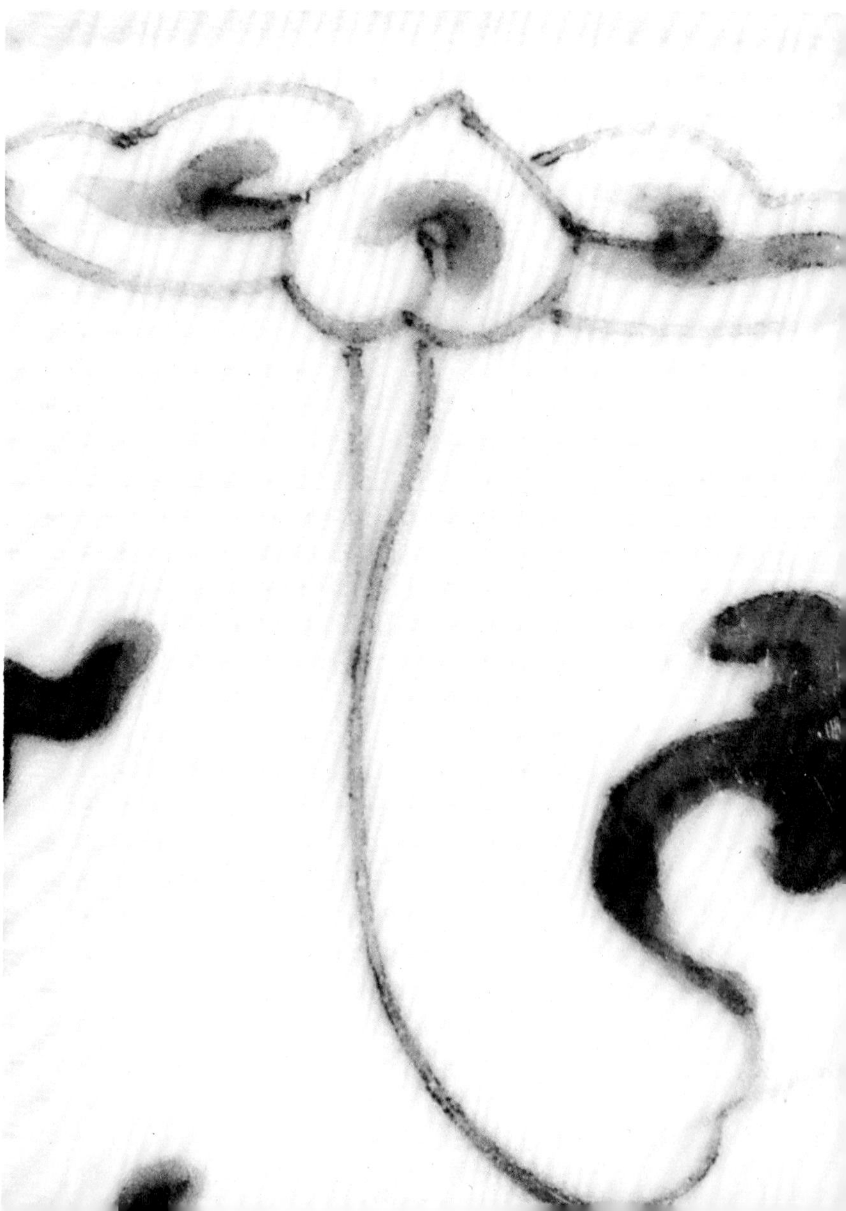

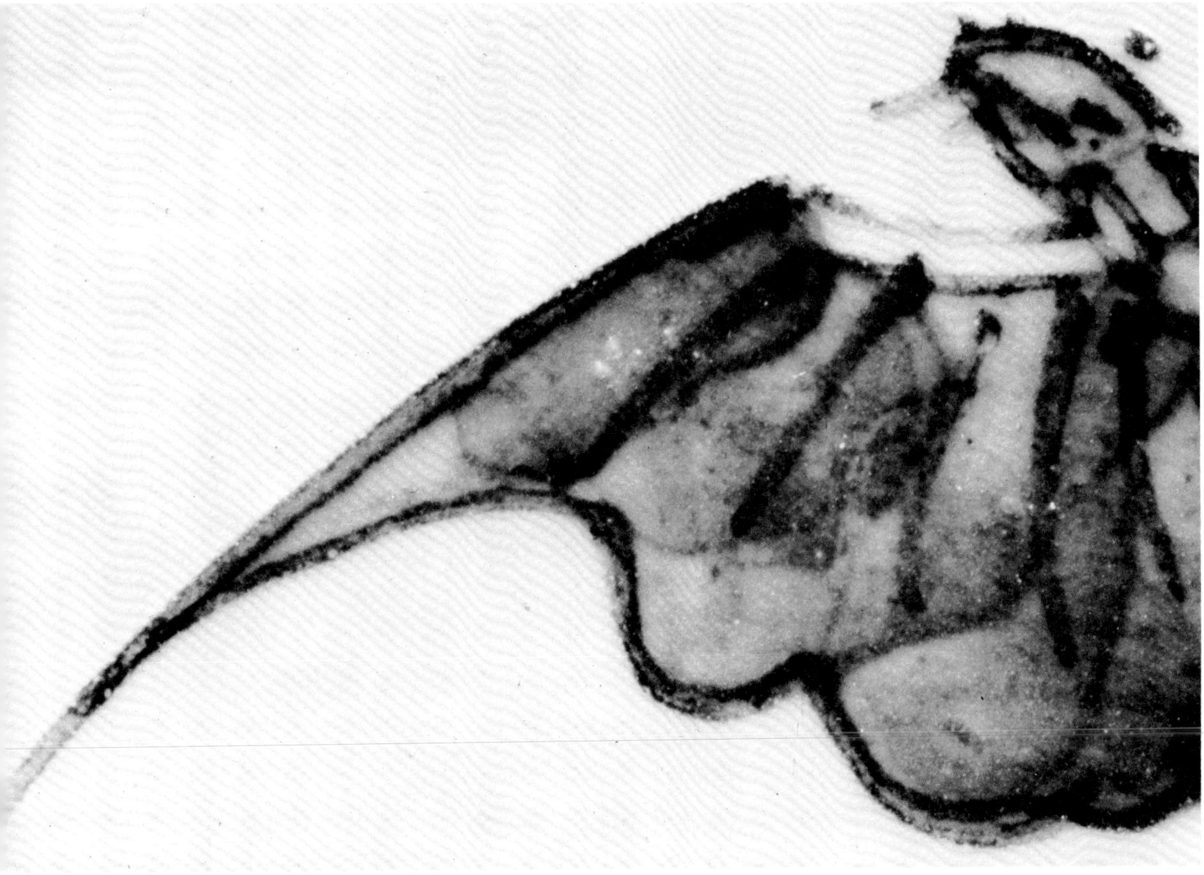

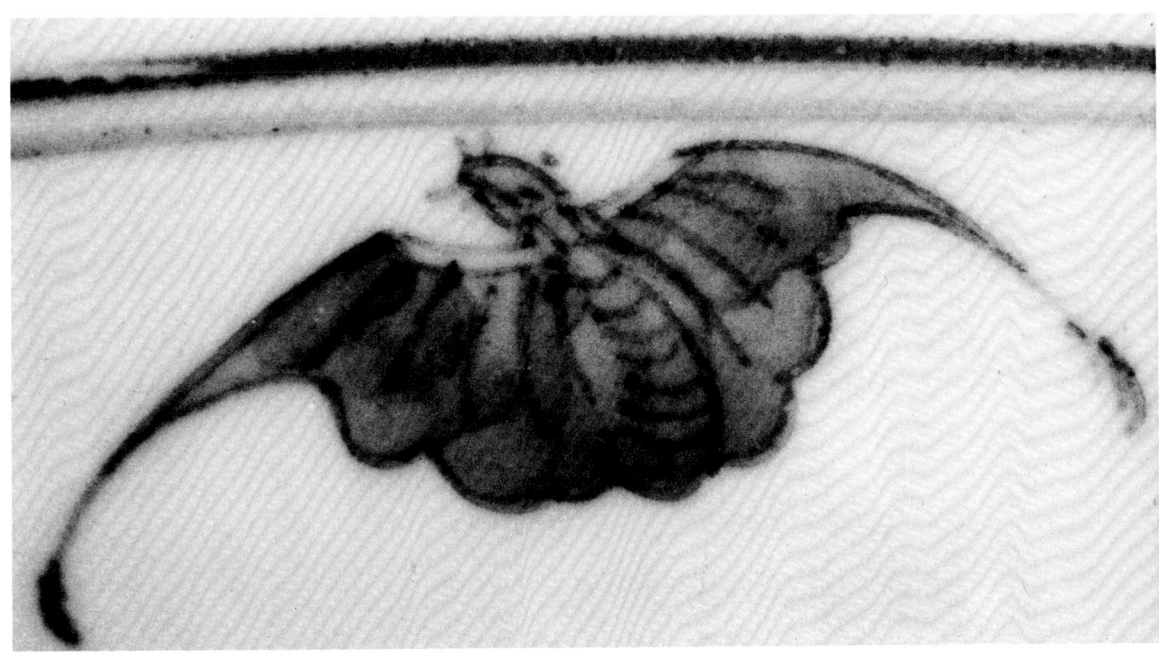

21

22

21 Detail. Bat wing with *hollow line* features. Blue and White Dish, pine tree and bats, six-character mark of Kuang Hsu (1875-1908). Interior of dish is similar to example in Van Oort, *Chinese Porcelain of the 19th and 20th Centuries,* p. 54, pl. 68.

22 Detail. Whole bat, from dish in Plate 21. Width between wing tips: 1¾."

23 Detail. Bamboo, on Blue and White Bowl, with decoration of the "three friends," prunus, bamboo and pine; six-character mark of Kuang Hsu (1875-1908). Private collection.

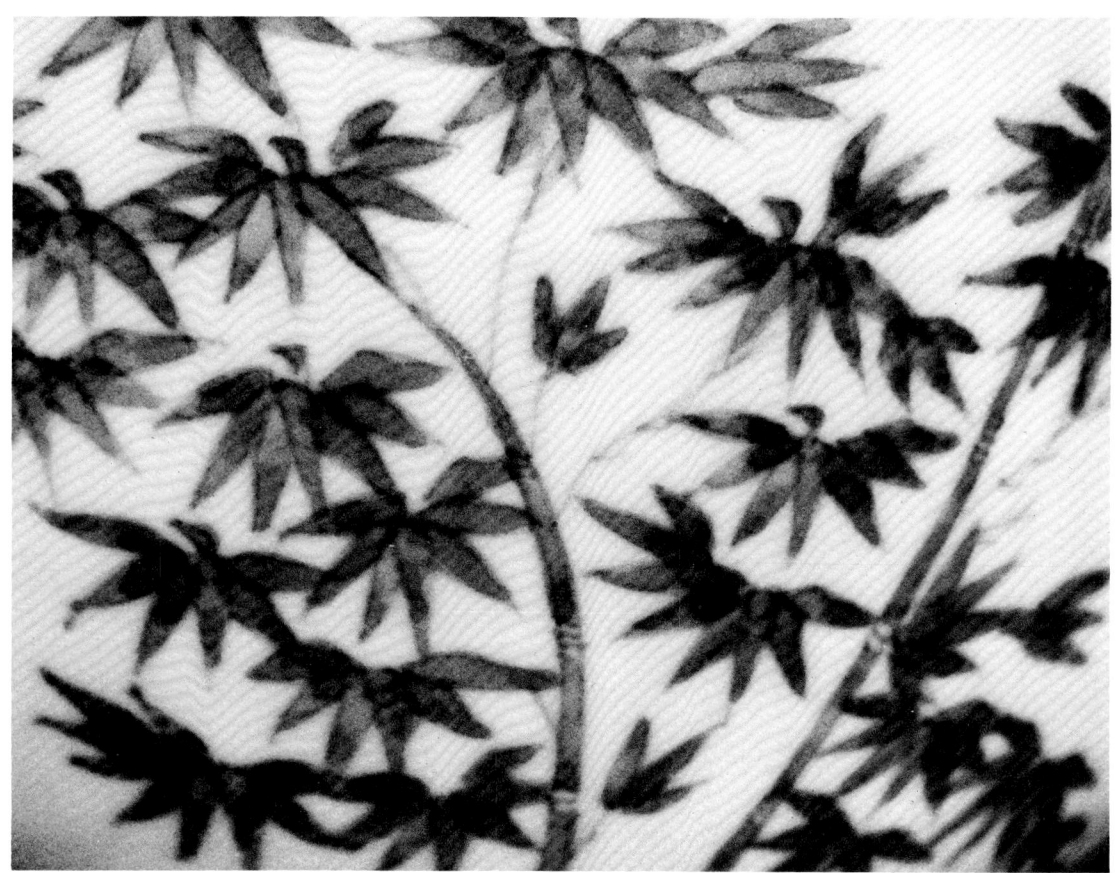

23

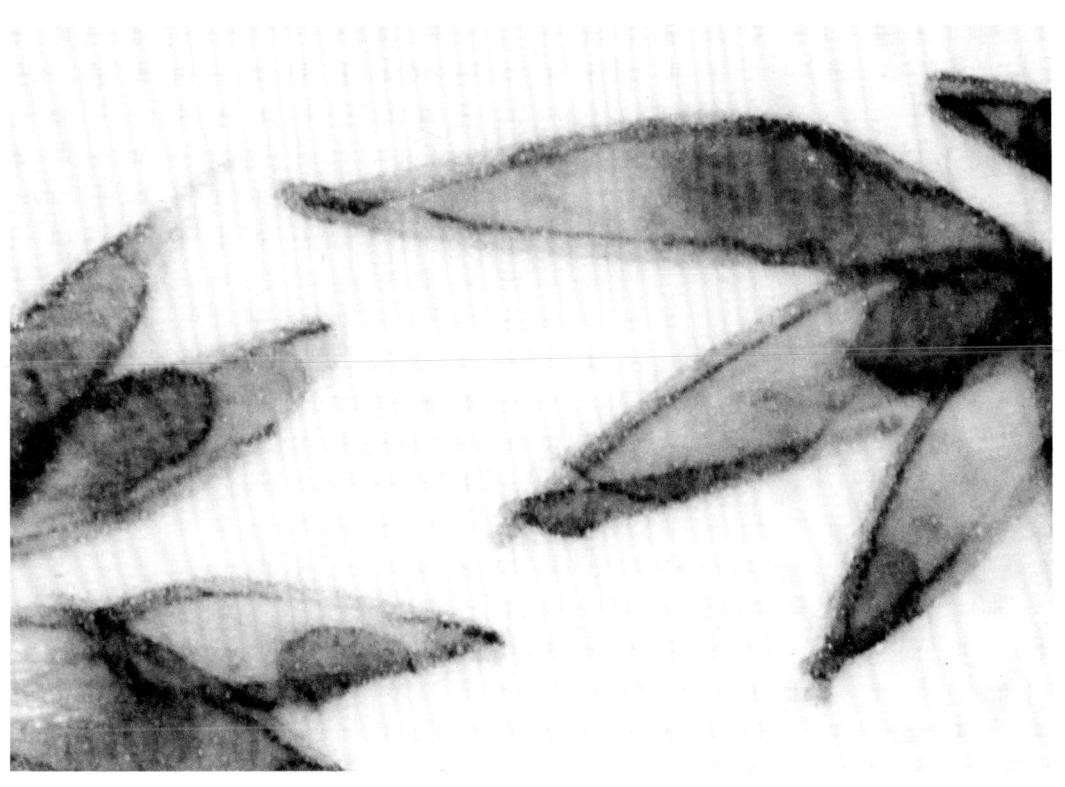

24　Detail. Bamboo leaves with *hollow lines,* color wash over outlining of leaves. From bowl in Plate 23.

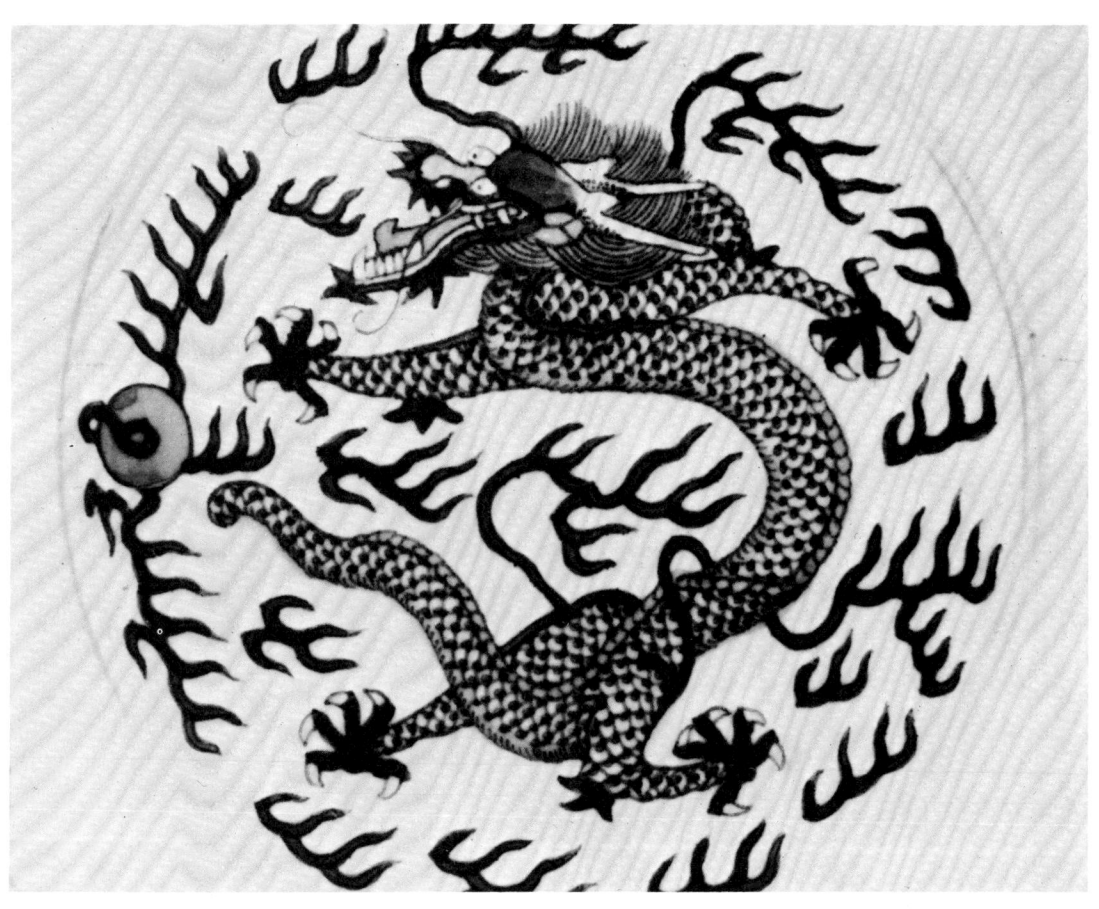

25   Detail. Dragon in center of Blue and White Dish, six-character mark of Kuang Hsu (1875-1908). 1½" H., 6½" D. See plates 26-28, 35-36, 50b. Private collection. Similar dishes in:

        a.   Munsterberg, *Dragons in Chinese Art*, p. 58,
               no. 60, Yung Cheng mark.
        b.   Sotheby Parke Bernet Catalogue, Hong Kong,
               May 19, 1977, no. 519, Tao Kuang seal mark.
        c.   _____ , New York,
               Sept. 23, 1976, no. 338, Hsien Feng mark.

26 Detail. Claw with *hollow line* nails. Nails: 1/8" H. From dish in Plates 25, 27-28, 35-36, 50b.

27 Detail. Eyes of dragon, 1/8" wide. Bubble in dot. Dot looks like a ring.

28 Detail. Horns of dragons with "rings."

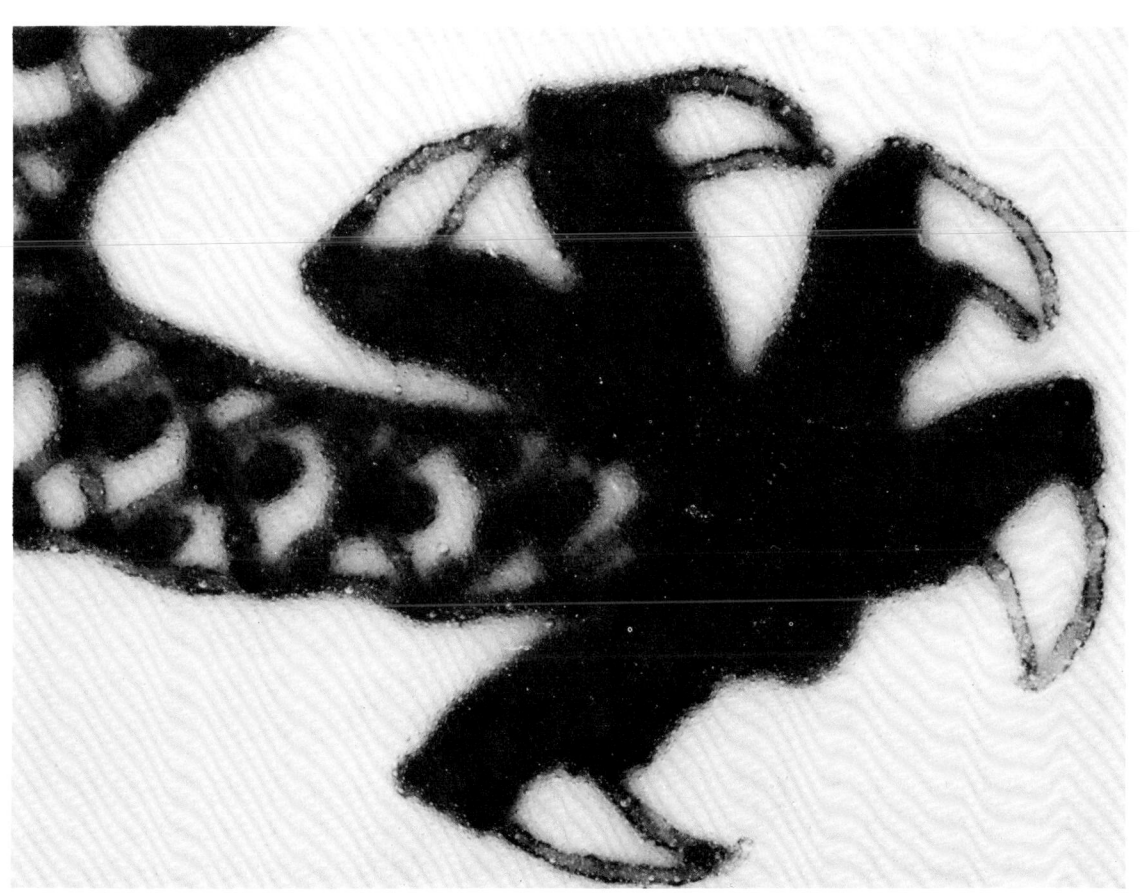

26

27

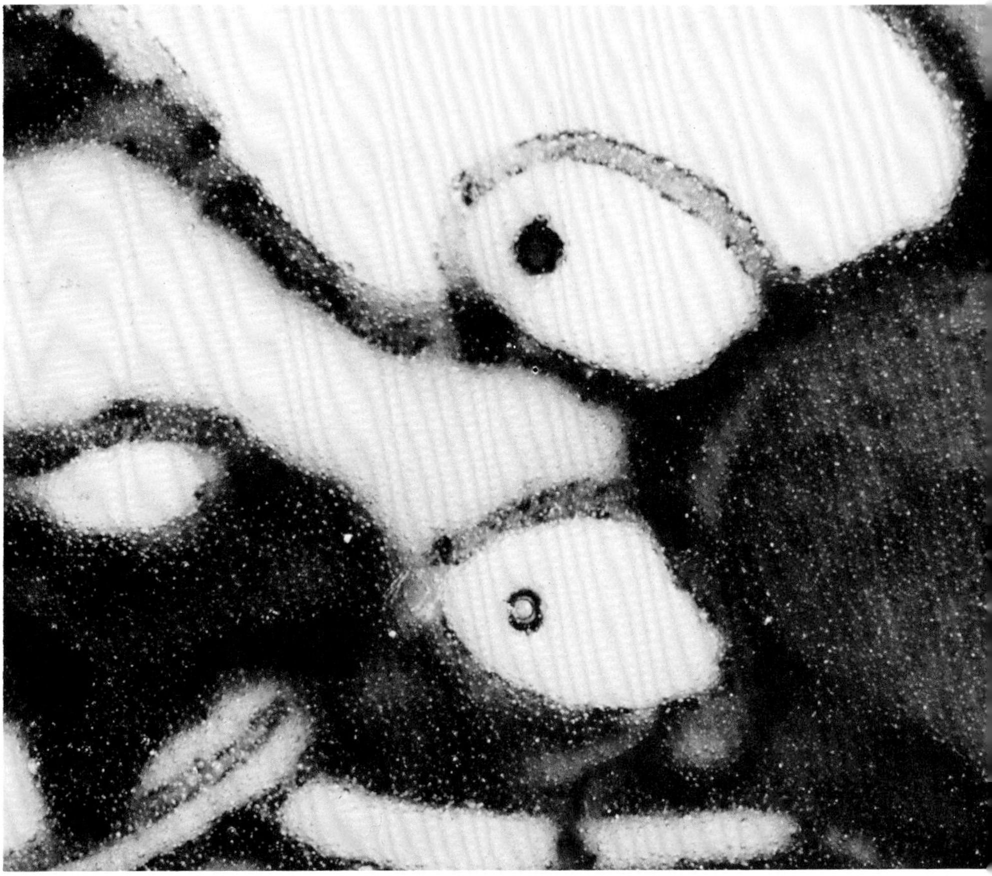

28

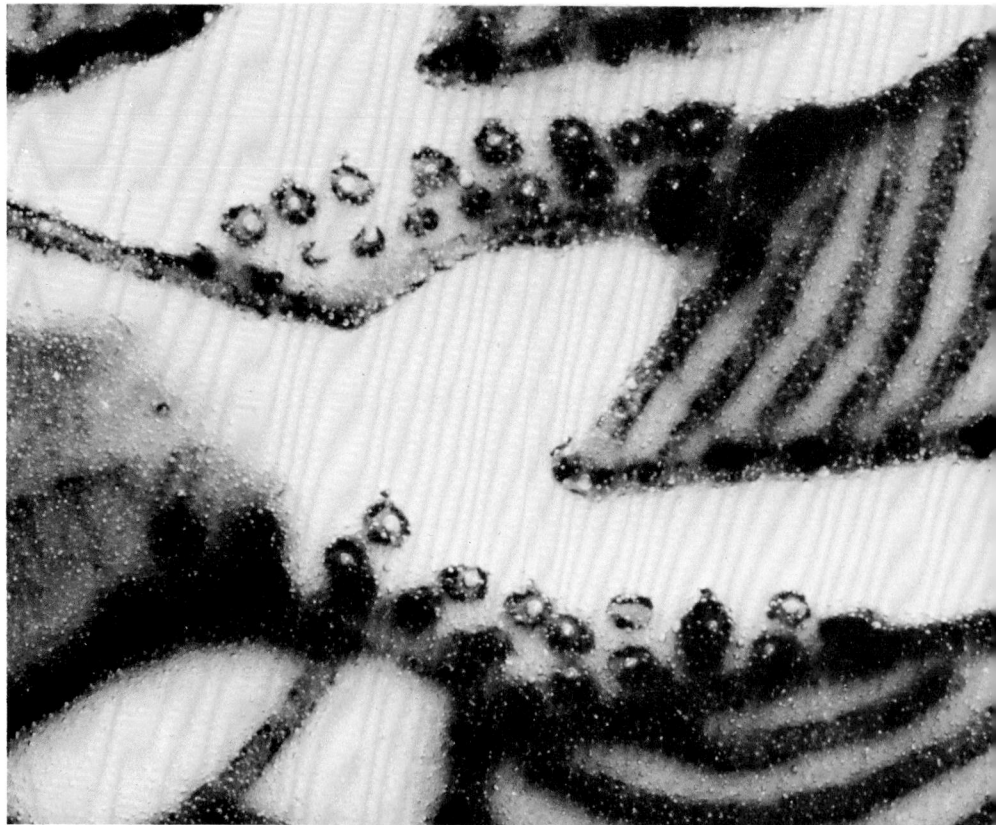

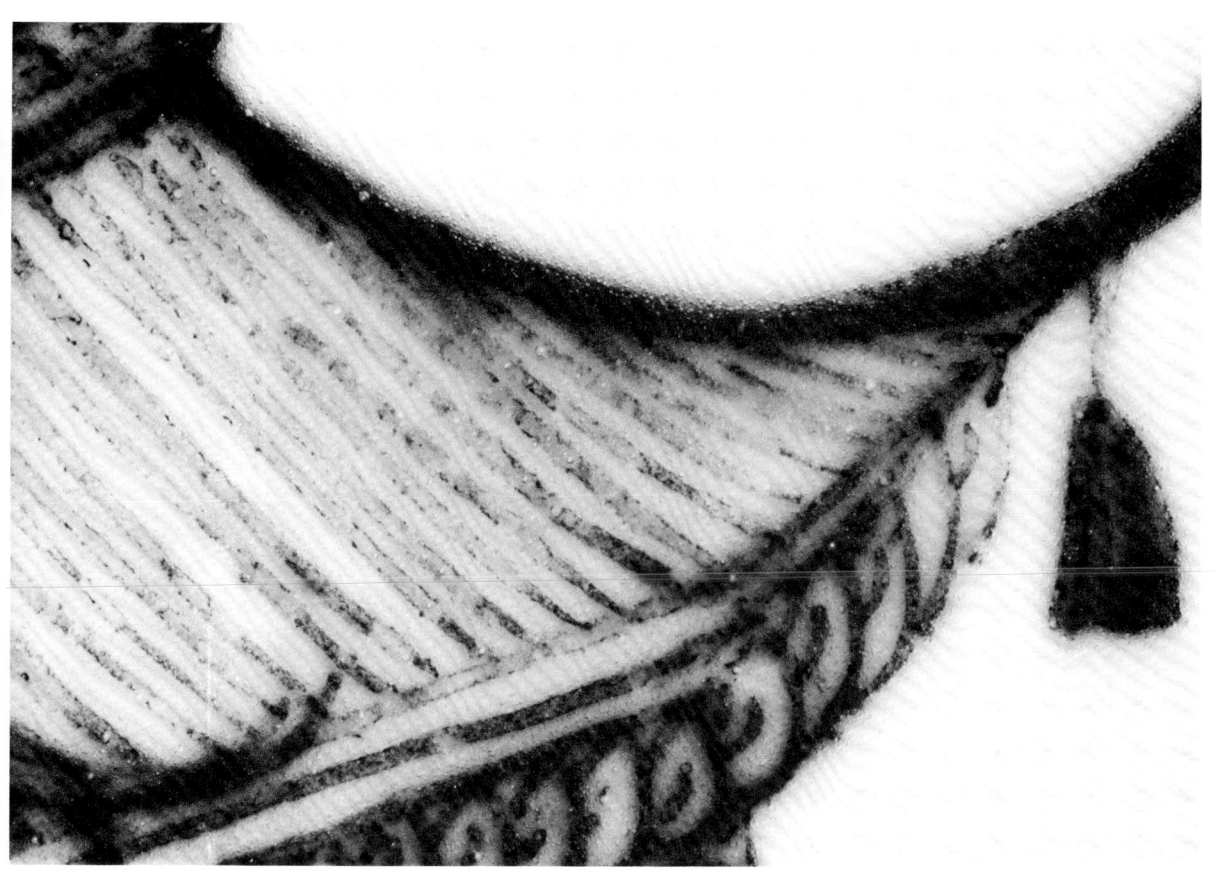

29

29 Detail. Roof with *hollow line* characteristic. From Blue and White Plaque in Plate 30.

30 Detail. Blue and White Plaque, considered late 19th century. Private collection.

31 Detail. Hawker, diluted blue lines, with features of the *hollow line.* From Plaque in Plates 29-30.

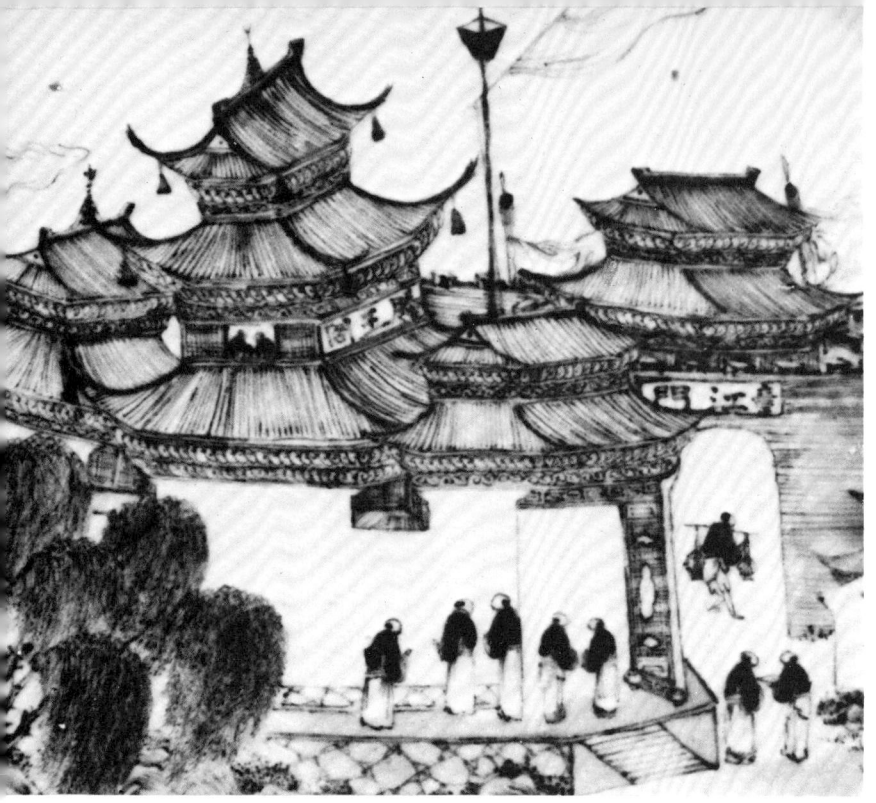

30

31

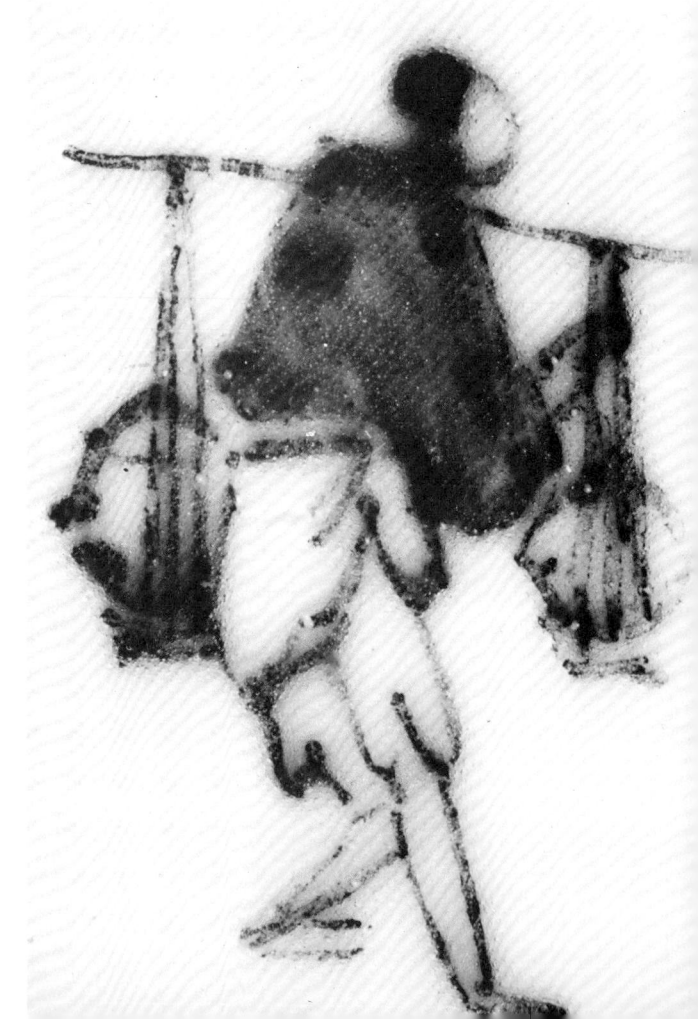

32 Blue and White Teapot, K'ang Hsi (1662-1772). 4½" H., 6½" W. Collection of the Asian Art Museum of San Francisco, The Avery Brundage Collection, no. B60 P1730.

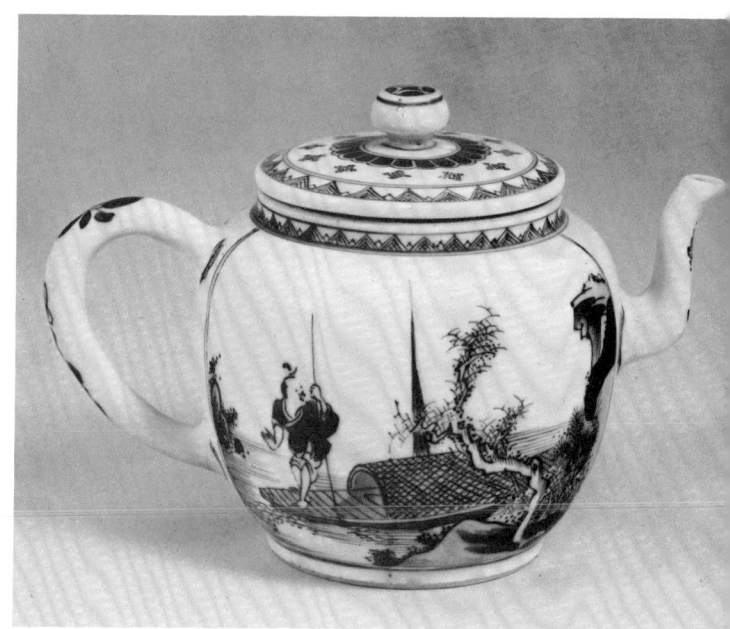

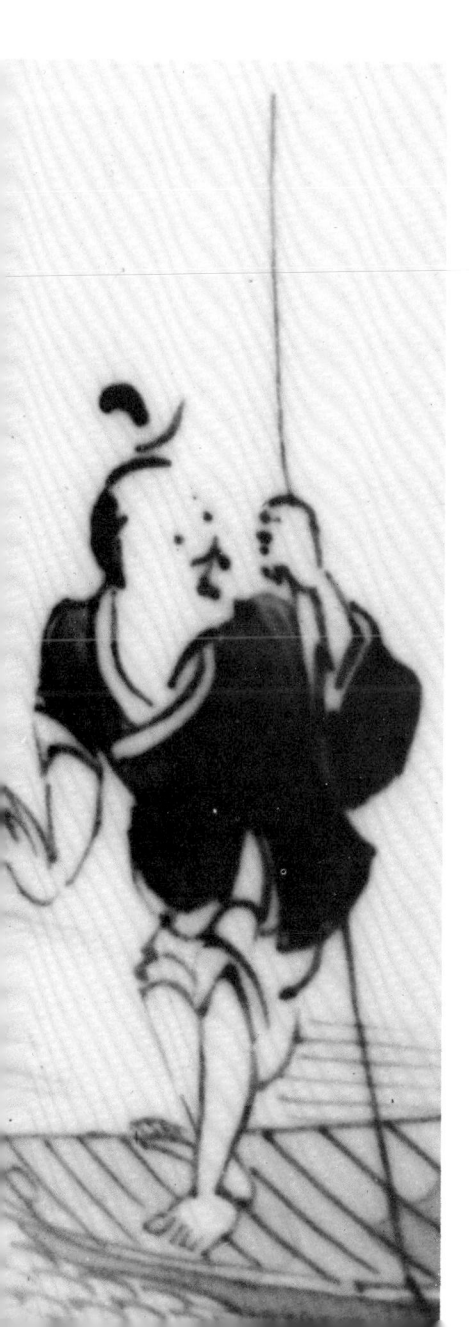

33 Detail. Fisherman painted with thin lines, all solid, homogeneous in color. From Teapot above.

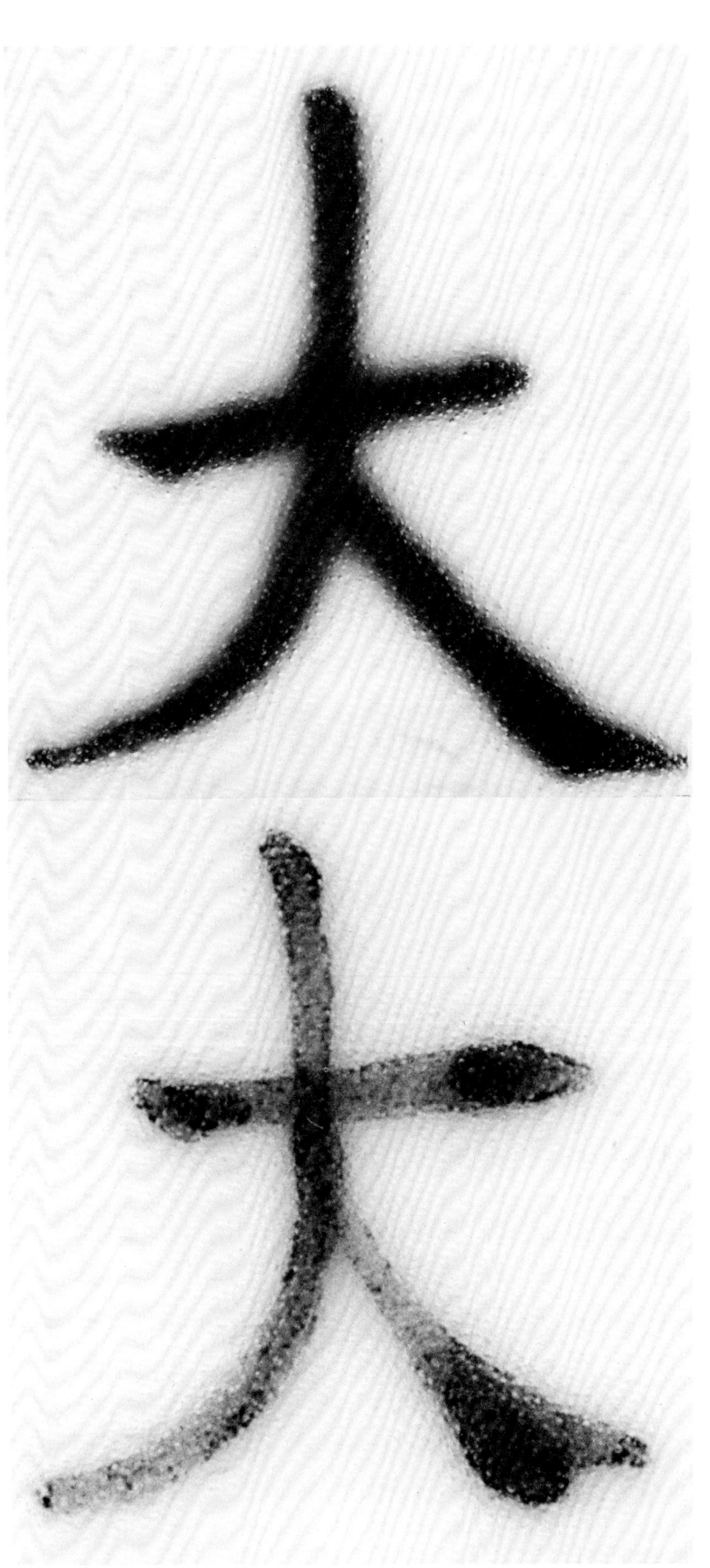

34

35

Plate 36

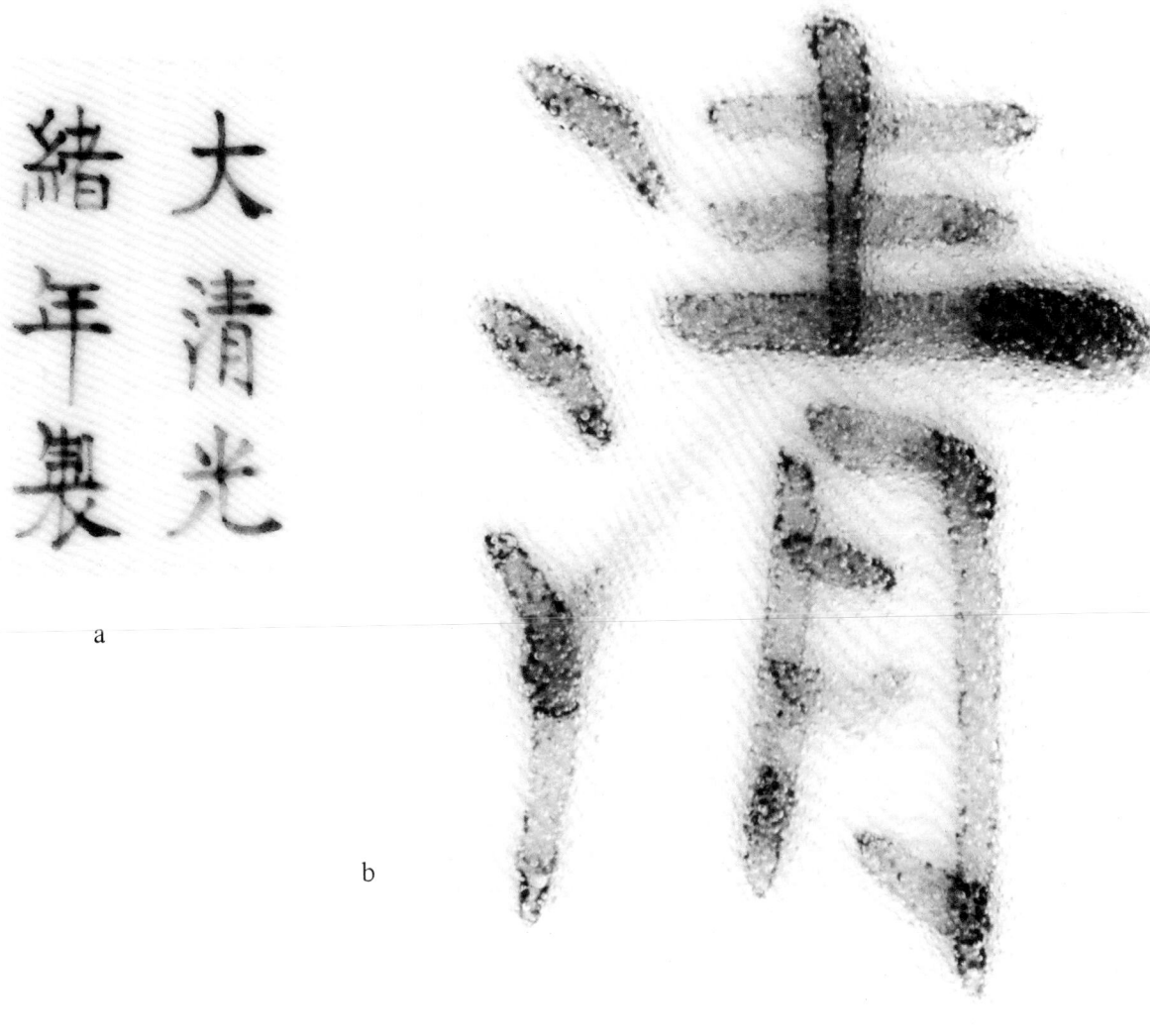

a

b

34 Detail. "Ta," solid lines, from six-character mark of Kuang Hsu (1875-1908). See Plates 37, 50c.

35 Detail. "Ta," *hollow line* character, from Kuang Hsu Dish in Plates 25-28, 36, 50b.

36a Underglaze blue six-character mark of Kuang Hsu (1875 - 1908) from Blue and White Dragon Design Plate.

36b Enlargement of "Ch'ing" from the above mark, with distinct *hollow lines.* See Plates 25 - 28, 35, 50b.

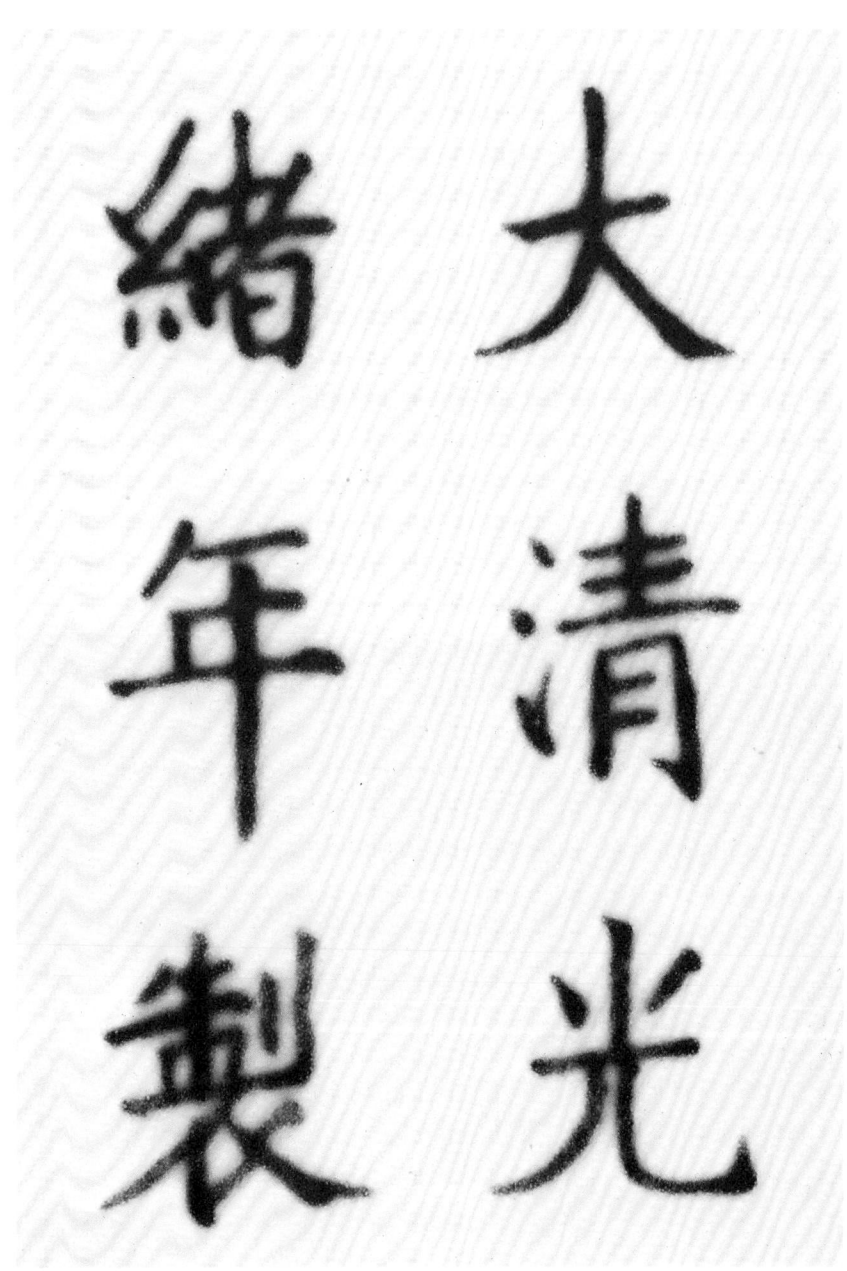

37   Detail. Underglaze blue six-character mark of Kuang Hsu (1875-1908), solid lines, homogeneous in color. From a *Famille-rose* Food Warmer, in three sections, with decor of peach tree, bats and dragons, 6½" H. See plates 34, 50c. Collection of Dr. Steven Wissig, San Francisco.

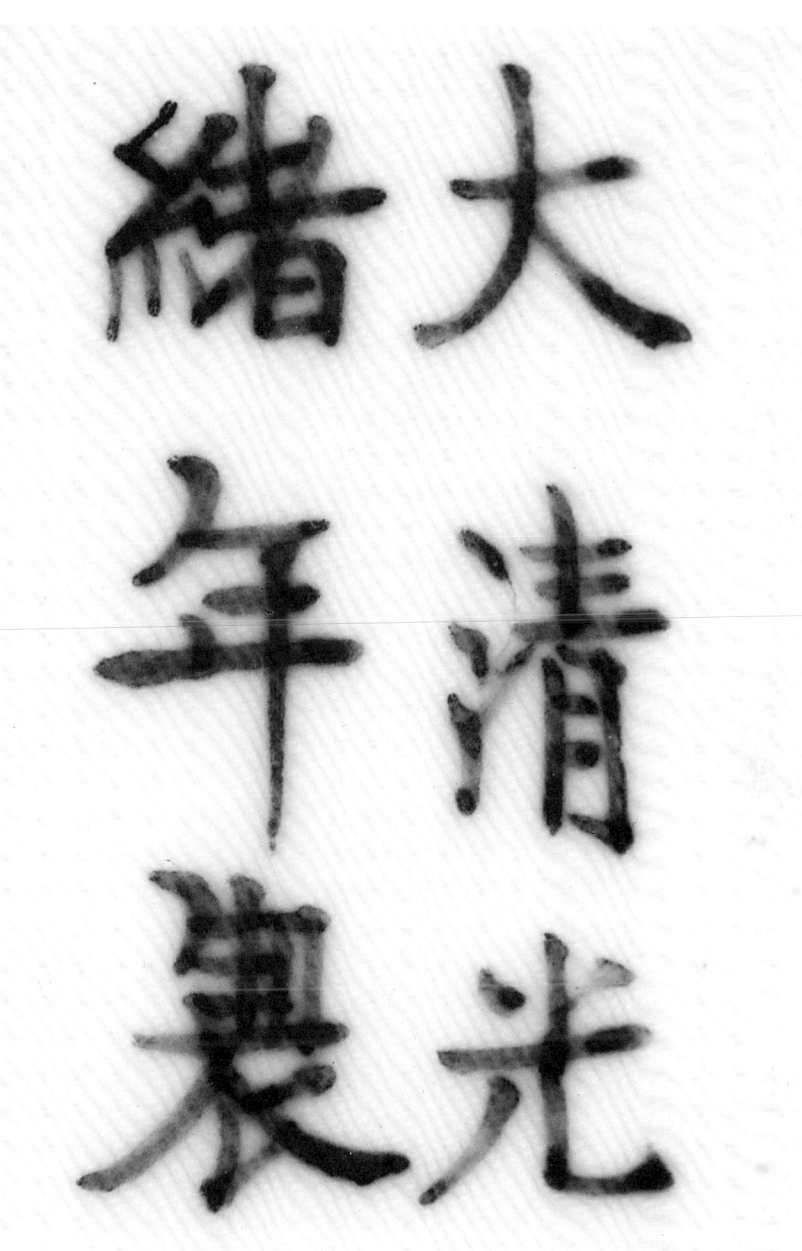

38 Detail. Underglaze six-character mark of Kuang Hsu, *hollow line* type. From a *Famille-rose* Plate, floral decor. 2" H., 8-1/8" D. See Plate 50d. Collection of Oriental Porcelain Gallery, San Francisco.

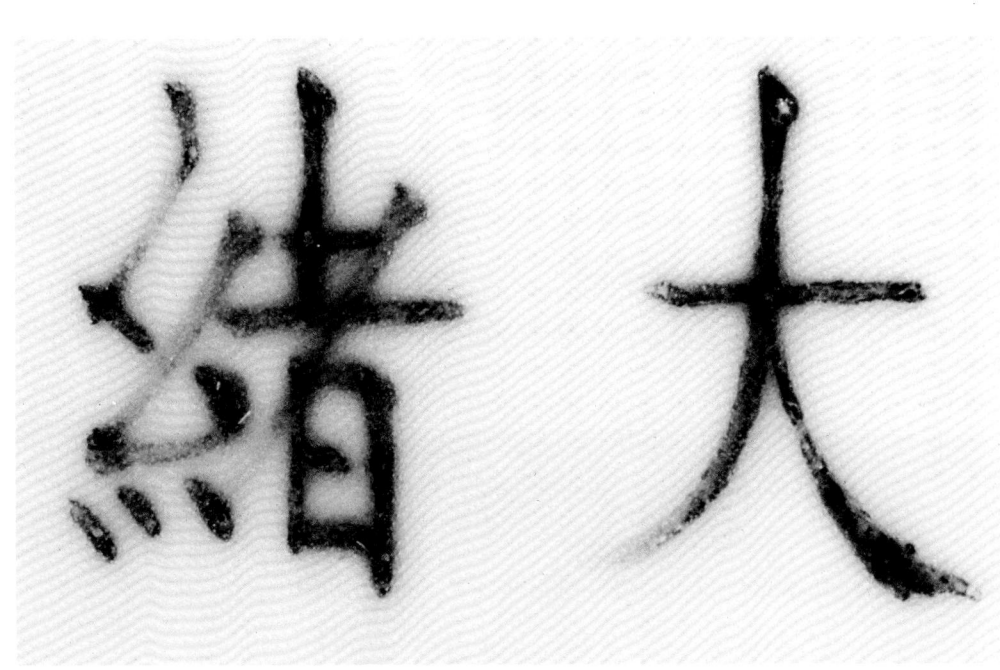

39   Detail, "Ta" and "Hsu" from six-character mark of the Ch'ing Dynasty Kuang
     Hsu period (1875-1908) in Plate 40. Blue and White Bowl with winged dragons
     and mythological animals above crested, swirling waves. See discussion on
     "Winged Dragons" in the following pages, also Notes II, no. 1, and Plates 50e,
     52-59. Collection of Wu Shu-Chen, San Francisco.

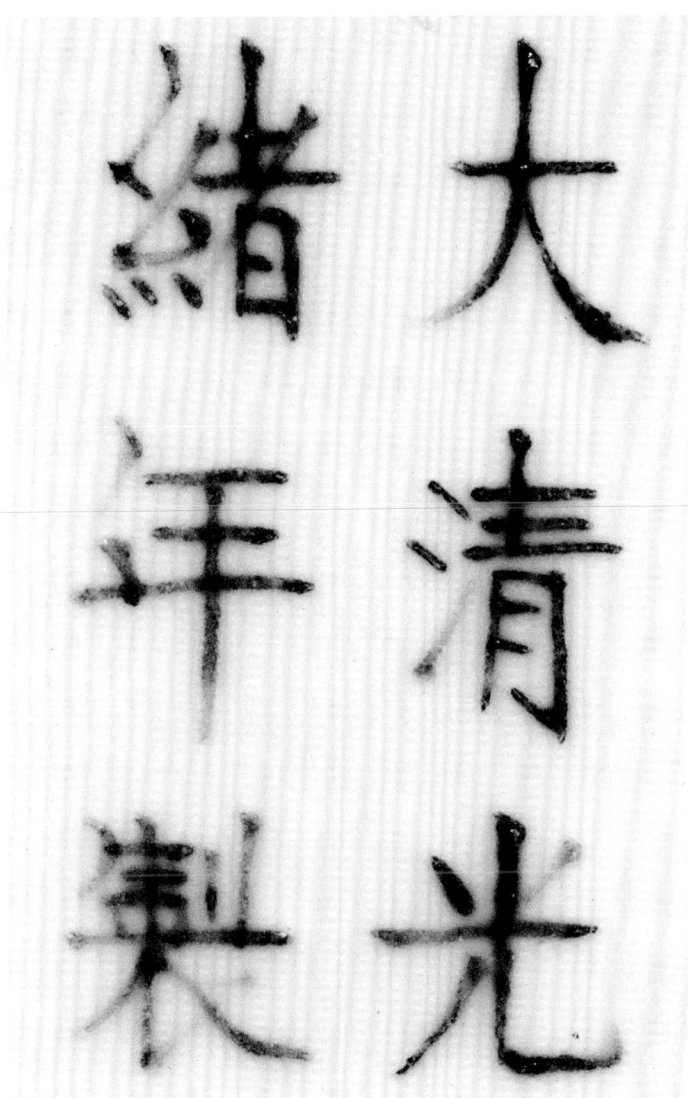

40   Detail. Six-character mark of Kuang Hsu (1875-1908), *hollow line* type. From
Blue and White Bowl with decoration almost entirely of *hollow lines* in Plates
50e, 51-59.

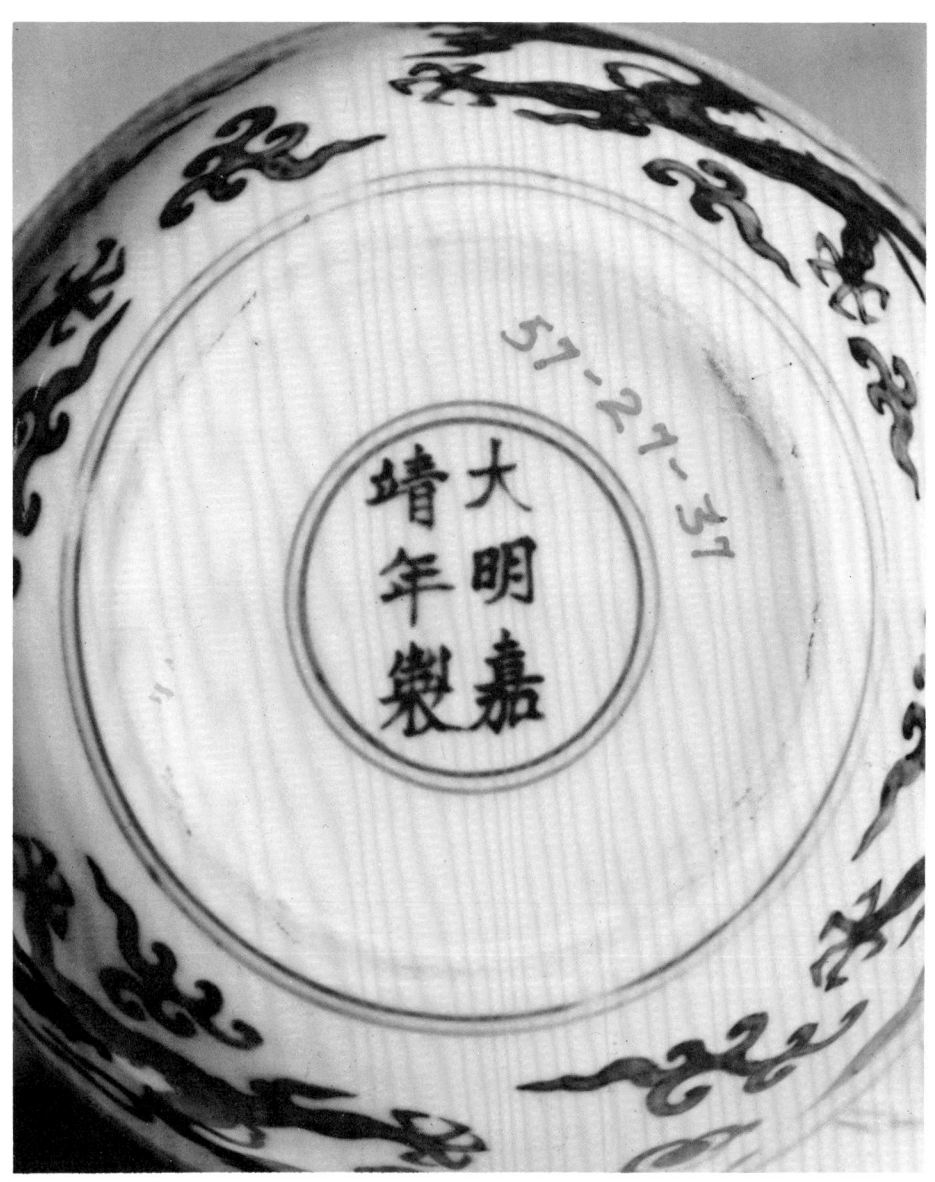

41 Detail. Six-character mark of Ming Dynasty Chia Ching (1522-66), light blue, solid lines, homogeneous in color. Blue and White Bowl. 5¼" D. Collection of the Asian Art Museum of San Francisco. The Roy Leventritt Collection, no. B69 P38L.

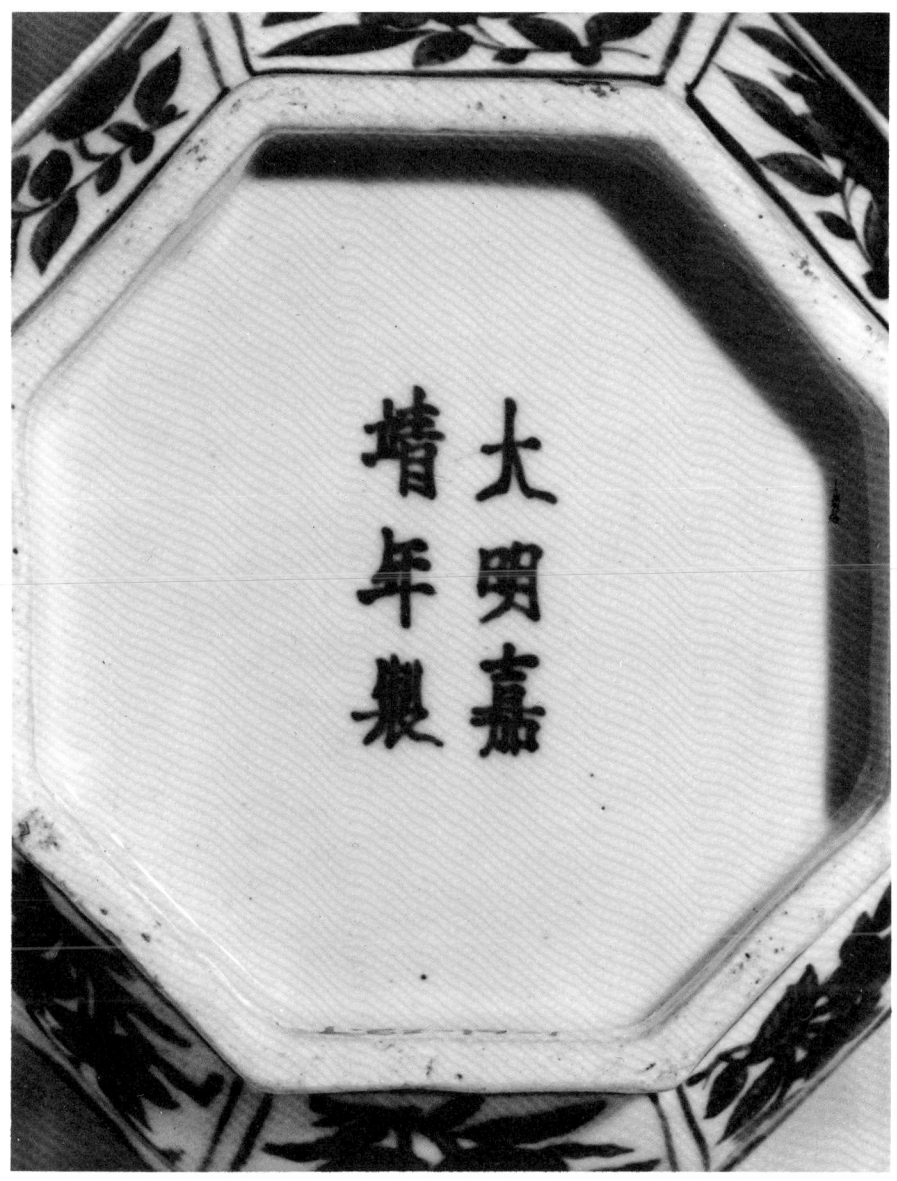

42   Detail. Six-character mark of Ming Dynasty Chia Ching (1522-66), dark blue, solid lines, homogeneous in color. Blue and White Octagonal Box. 5½" W. Collection of the Asian Art Museum of San Francisco, The Roy Leventritt Collection, no. B69 P42L.

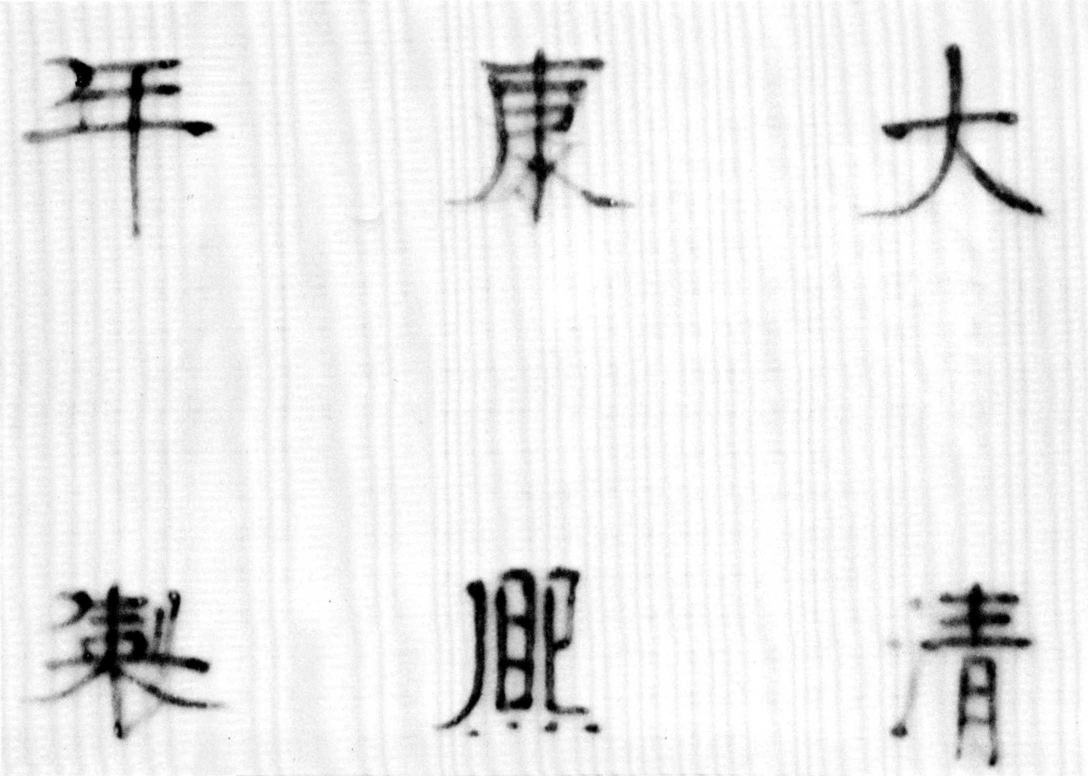

年 東 大

樂 熙 清

43

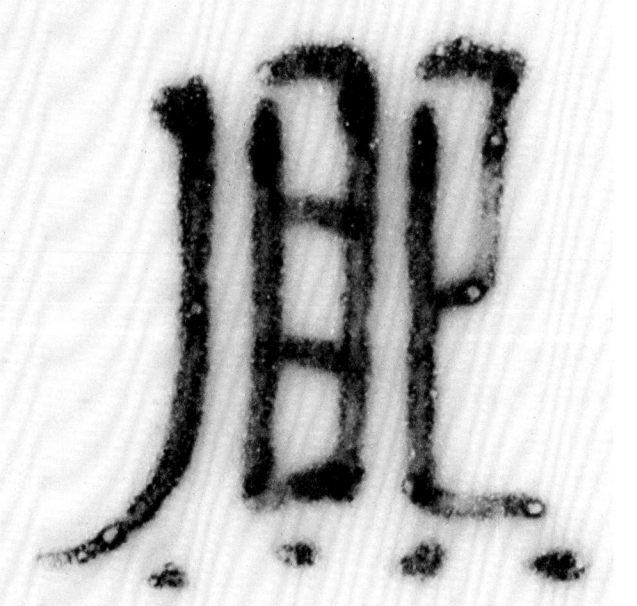

44

43 Detail. Six-character mark of K'ang Hsi.   White Beehive-shaped Waterpot. Considered 19th Century.   3¾" H., 5" D. See Notes I, no. 30 and Notes II, no. 46. Collection of G.T. Marsh and Company, San Francisco.

44 Detail. "Hsi," from K'ang Hsi mark in Plate 43. With accumulations in *hollow lines* and *rings.*

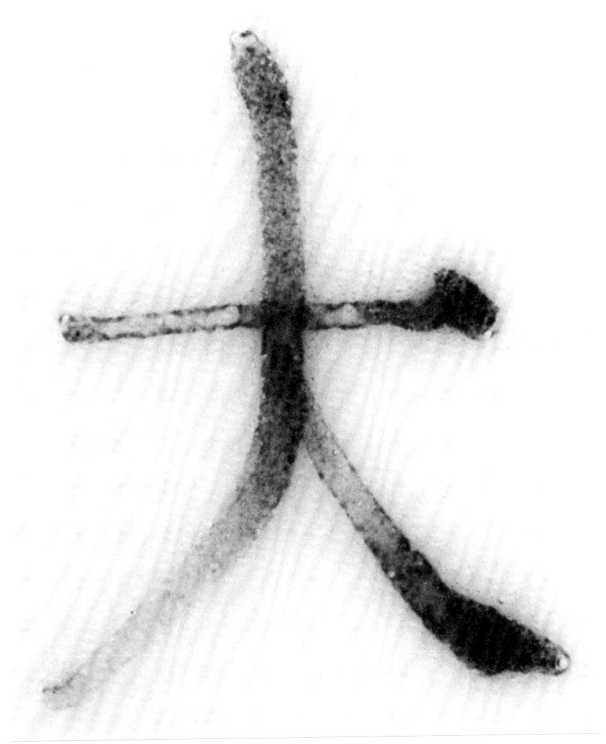

45   Detail. "Ta," with *hollow* and *split line* characteristics. From Plate 47.

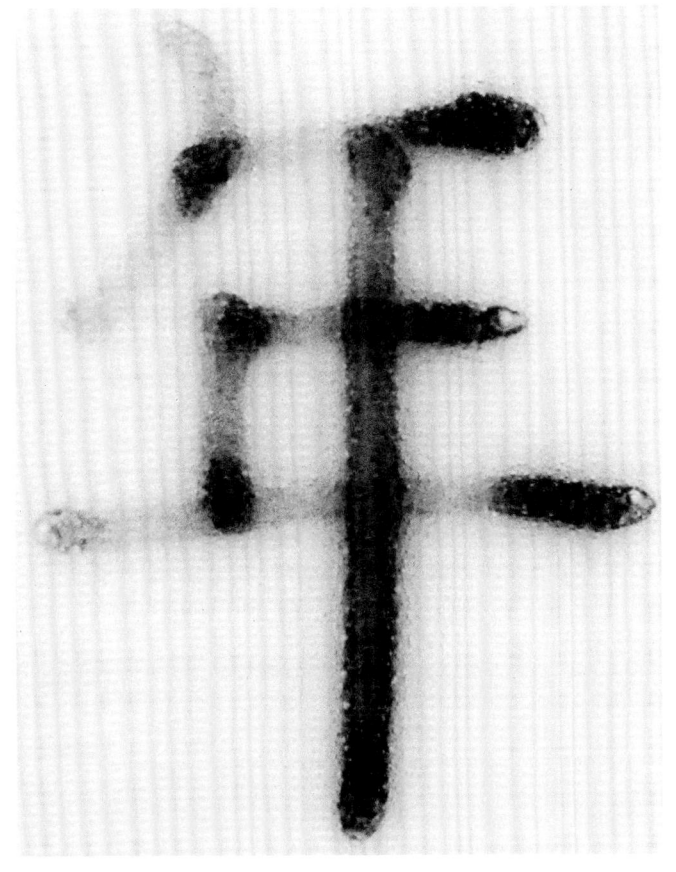

46   Detail. "Nien," with *hollow line* features. See Plate 47.

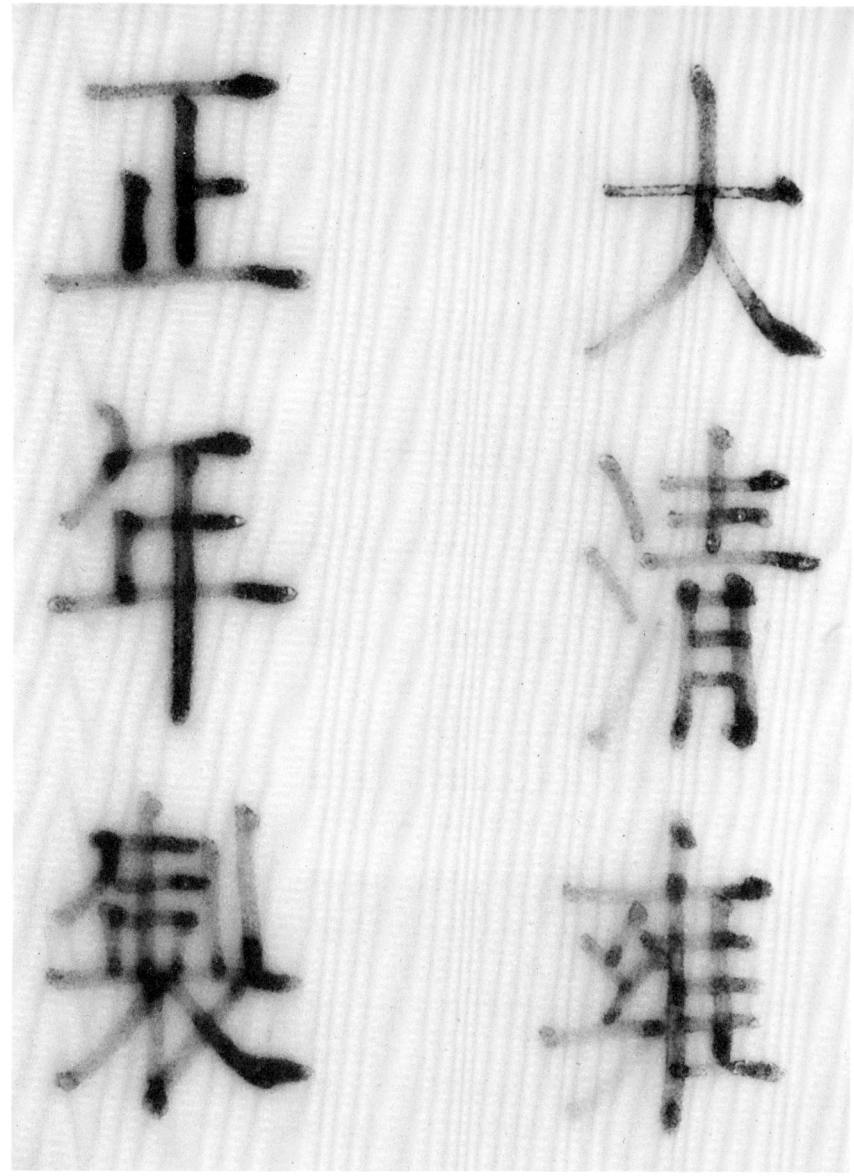

47 Detail. Six-character reign mark of Yung Cheng. Blue and White Saucer. See Plates 45 - 46. Compare this reign mark with the ones in Plates 40, 48, 50e and 50f. This saucer is an excellent example of finer quality Ch'ing Dynasty porcelain. The glaze is unctuous, and the biscuit is smooth. The decoration is a wave pattern on the outside. When holding this piece, hardly anyone would think that it is not a Yung Cheng period specimen. As a simple saucer, its fine appearance and reign mark give little reason for the observer to suspect it; the satisfaction and enjoyment of viewing it as an exemplary specimen would resist consideration of any suggestion that it may not be what it appears to be. On close examination, blemishes in the glaze, impurities in the biscuit, rigidity of the application of the diluted cobalt blue, and mechanical execution of the characters of the reign mark are details more commonly seen in the Kuang Hsu period (1875 - 1908) than in the Yung Cheng one (1723 - 35). Features of the *hollow line,* most frequently observed in Kuang Hsu period products, are visible in the brushstrokes also. This saucer, and others like it, is a subject of constant inquiry. Dated and documented specimens of all periods of the Ch'ing Dynasty help to more accurately identify such "perfectly beautiful" porcelains. 7/8" H., 4-1/8" D. Author's collection.

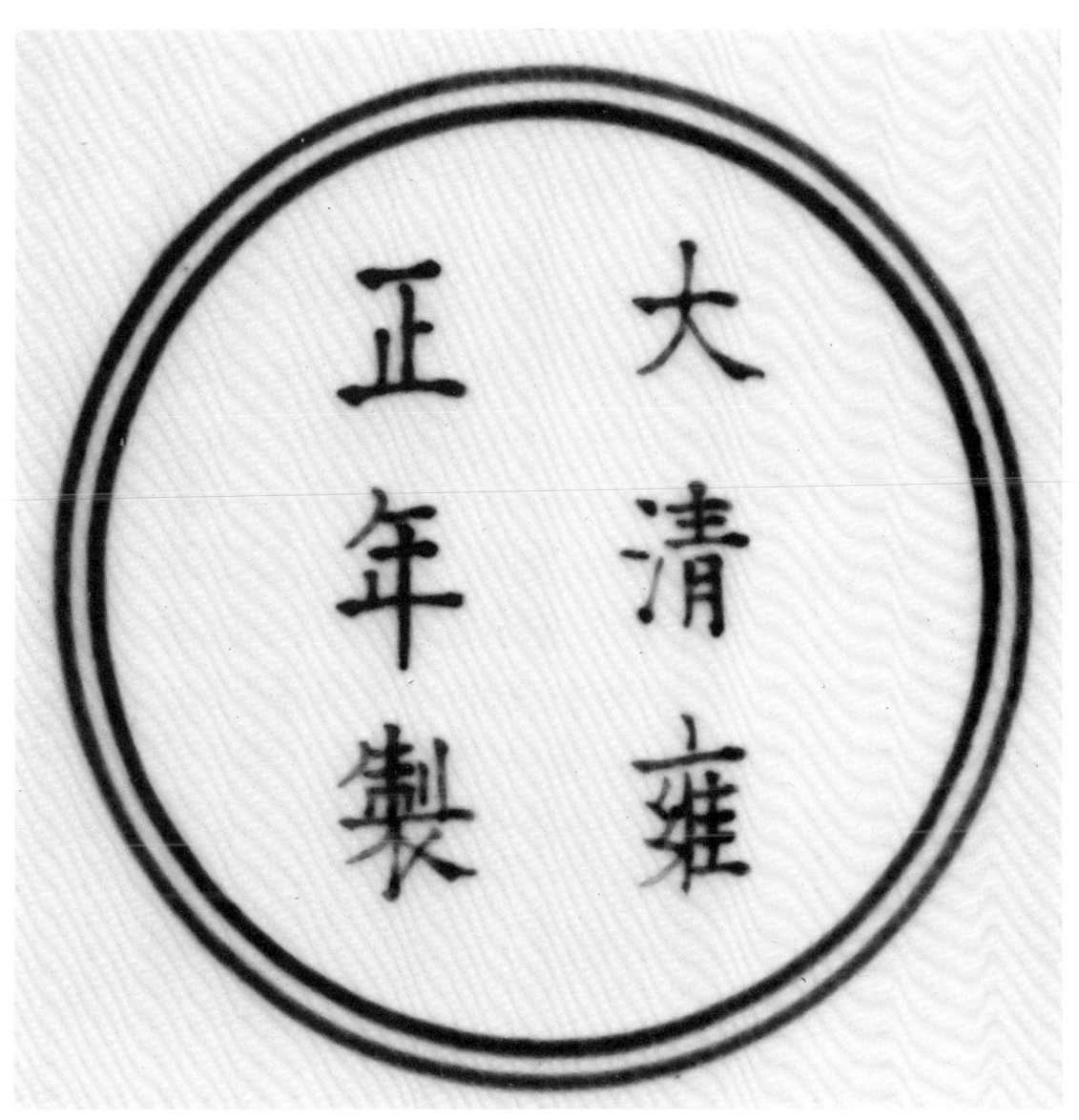

48   Detail. Yung Cheng mark from a Yung Cheng Platter (1723-35) in Plate 63.
Collection of the Asian Art Museum of San Francisco, The Avery Brundage
Collection, no. B60 P269.

49   Detail. Six-character seal mark of Chia Ch'ing. Blue and White
Bowl, floral decor.   Early 20th Century.   Private Collection.

Illustrations of entire specimens and their details in forthcoming
book *Dating Chinese Ceramics.*

50   a.   From Plate 49.

b.   From Plates 25-28, 35-36.

c.   From Plate 37.

d.   From Plate 38.

e.   From Plate 40.

f.   From Plate 47. Compare this with no. e.

Plate 50

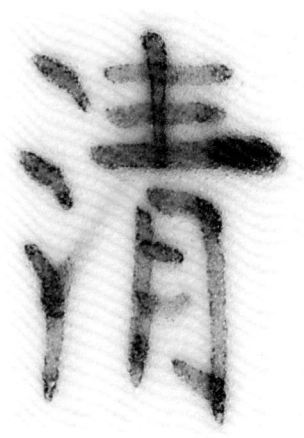

b

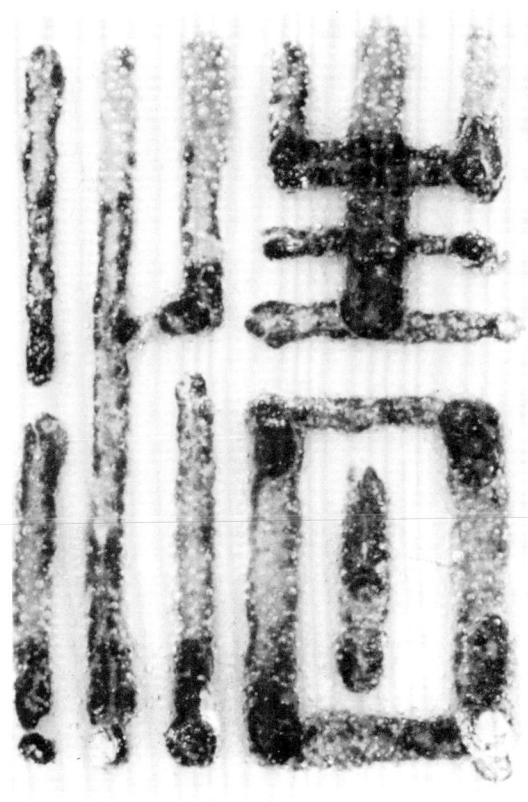

a

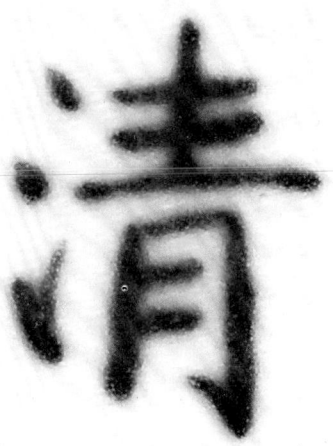

c

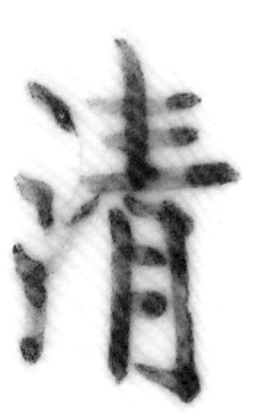

d

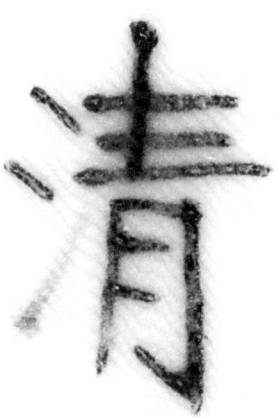

e

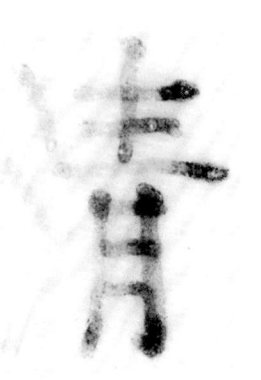

f

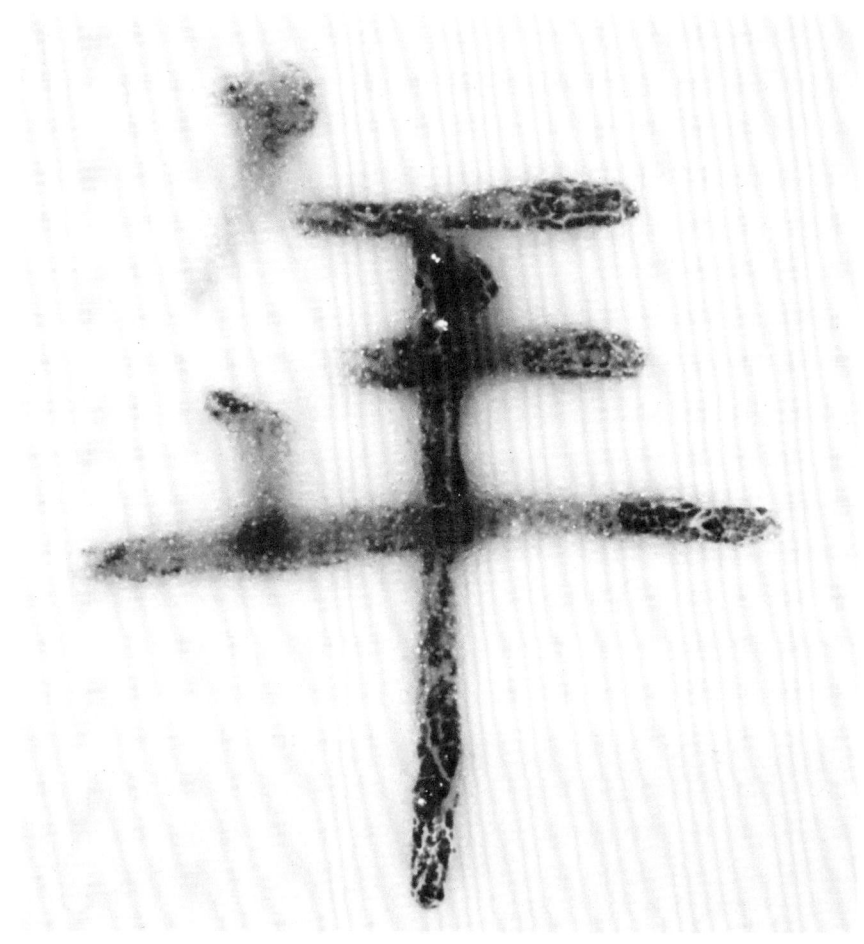

51

52 ⇨

51 Detail. "Nien," with *cracked line*. From six-character mark of the Kuang Hsu period (1875-1908). Blue and White Dish, lotus design. Private collection.

52 Detail. Wave pattern with *hollow lines*. Blue and White Bowl, mythological animals and winged dragons over crested, swirling waves, with six-character mark of Kuang Hsu (1875-1908). 3¾" H., 8-3/8" D. Actual area of this detail: 1-3/8" H., 1" W. See Plates 39-40, 50e, 53-59; Notes II, no. 1. Subjects of decoration discussed under "Winged Dragons." Collection of Wu Shu-Chen, San Francisco.

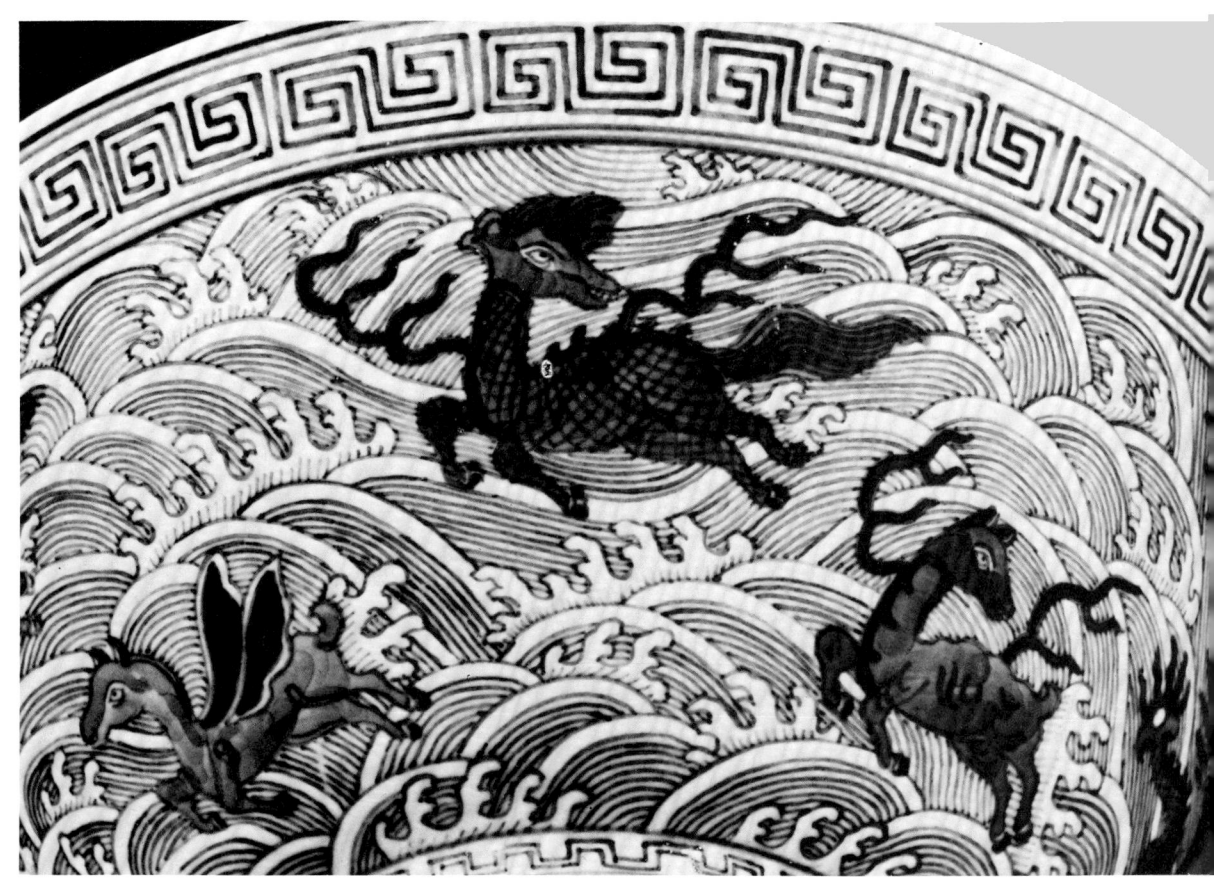

53   Detail. Mythological animals over crested, swirling waves between a mouth-rim band of ket-fret and a ring-foot band of dentil. From a distance, all lines look solid. Actually, almost every line has the *hollow line* characteristic. From a Blue and White Bowl, with a Kuang Hsu six-character mark (1875 - 1908). 3¾" H. 8-3/8" D. See Plates 39 - 40, 50e, 54 - 59, and Notes II, no. 1. Mythological animals and winged dragons discussed on pages 75 - 83. Collection of Wu Shu-Chen, San Francisco.

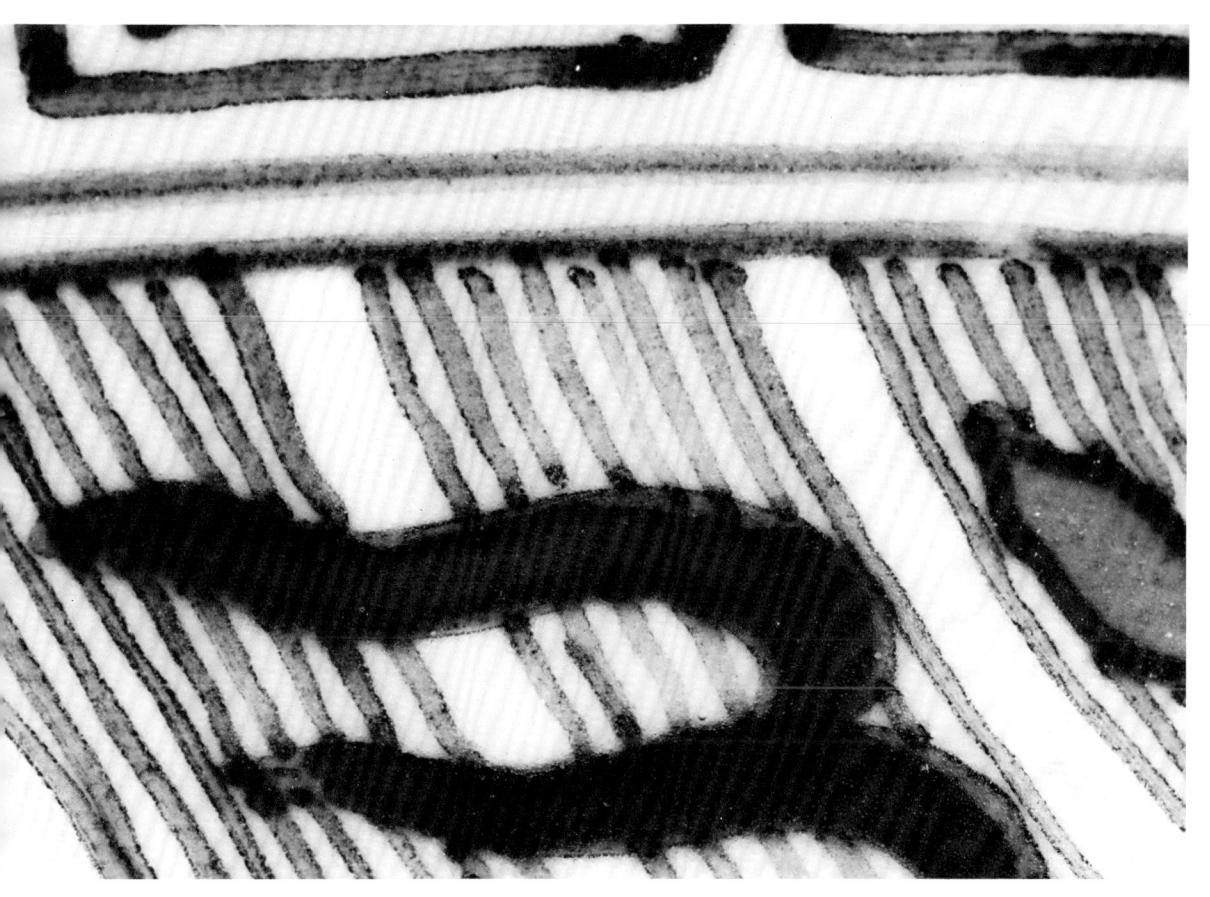

54 Detail. Wave pattern under key-fret band, with *hollow lines* and accumulations. Kuang Hsu Bowl in Plates 39-40, 50e, 52-53, 55-59.

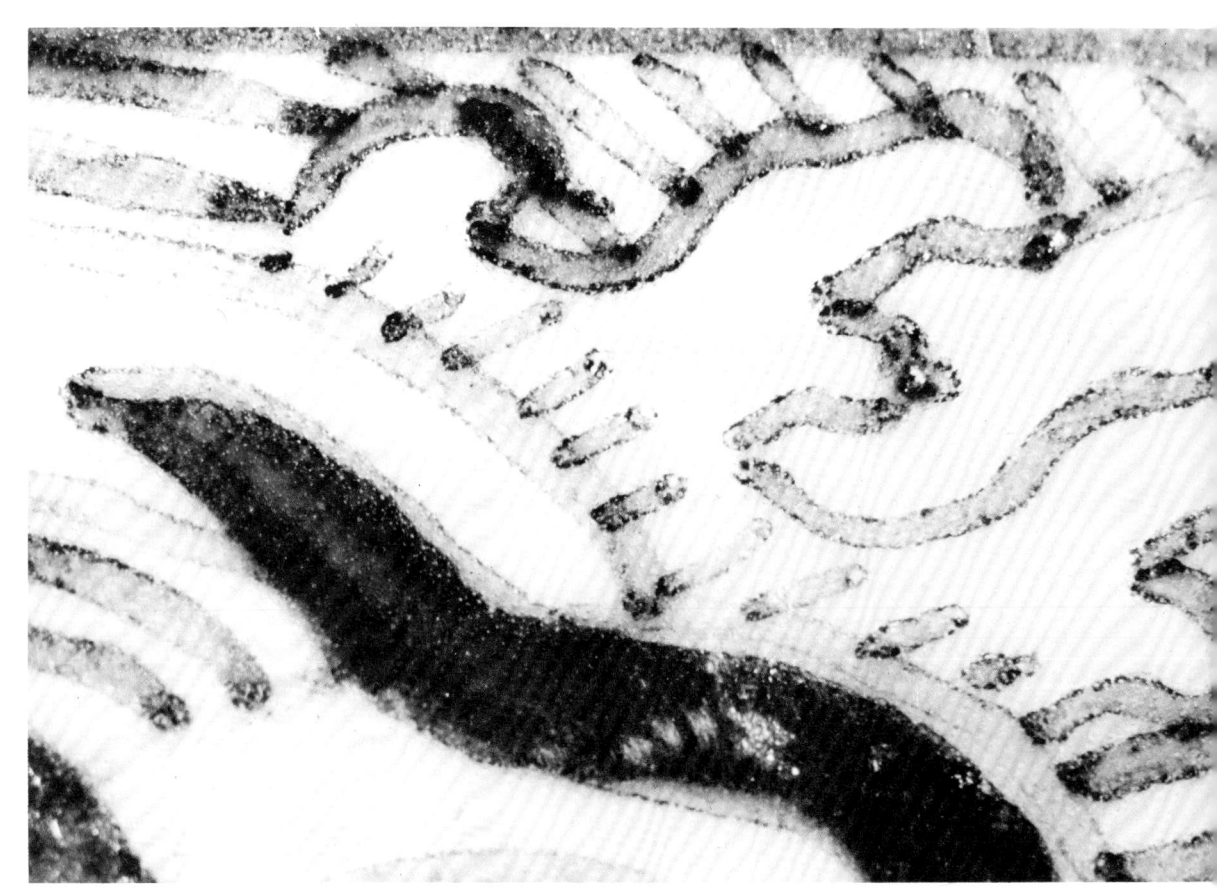

55 Detail. Wave pattern. In the center, *hollow lines* with *rings*. From bowl in Plates 39-40, 50e, 52-54, 56-59.

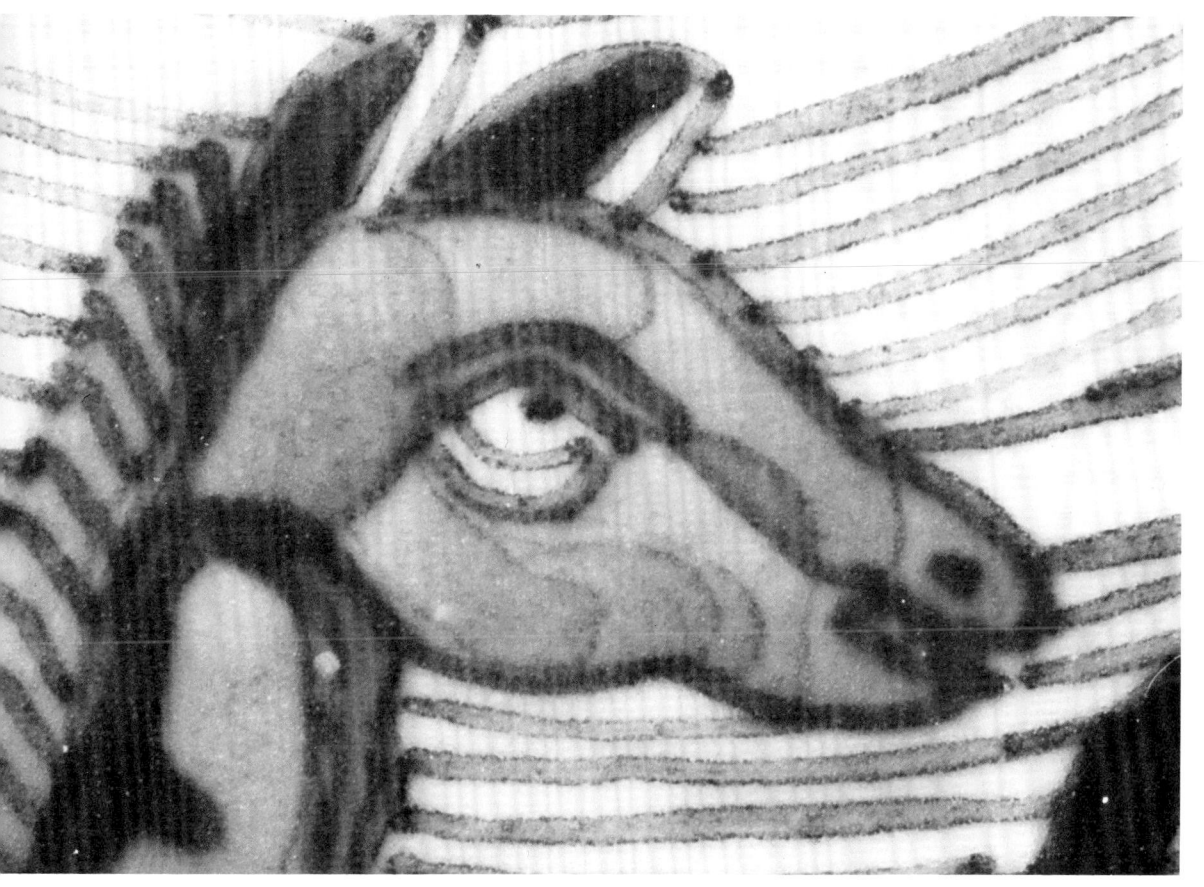

56 Detail. Head of horse with *hollow lines* and edge of color washes with distinct coincidental outline. From Kuang Hsu Bowl in Plates 39-40, 50e, 52-55, 57-59. Collection of Wu Shu-Chen, San Francisco.

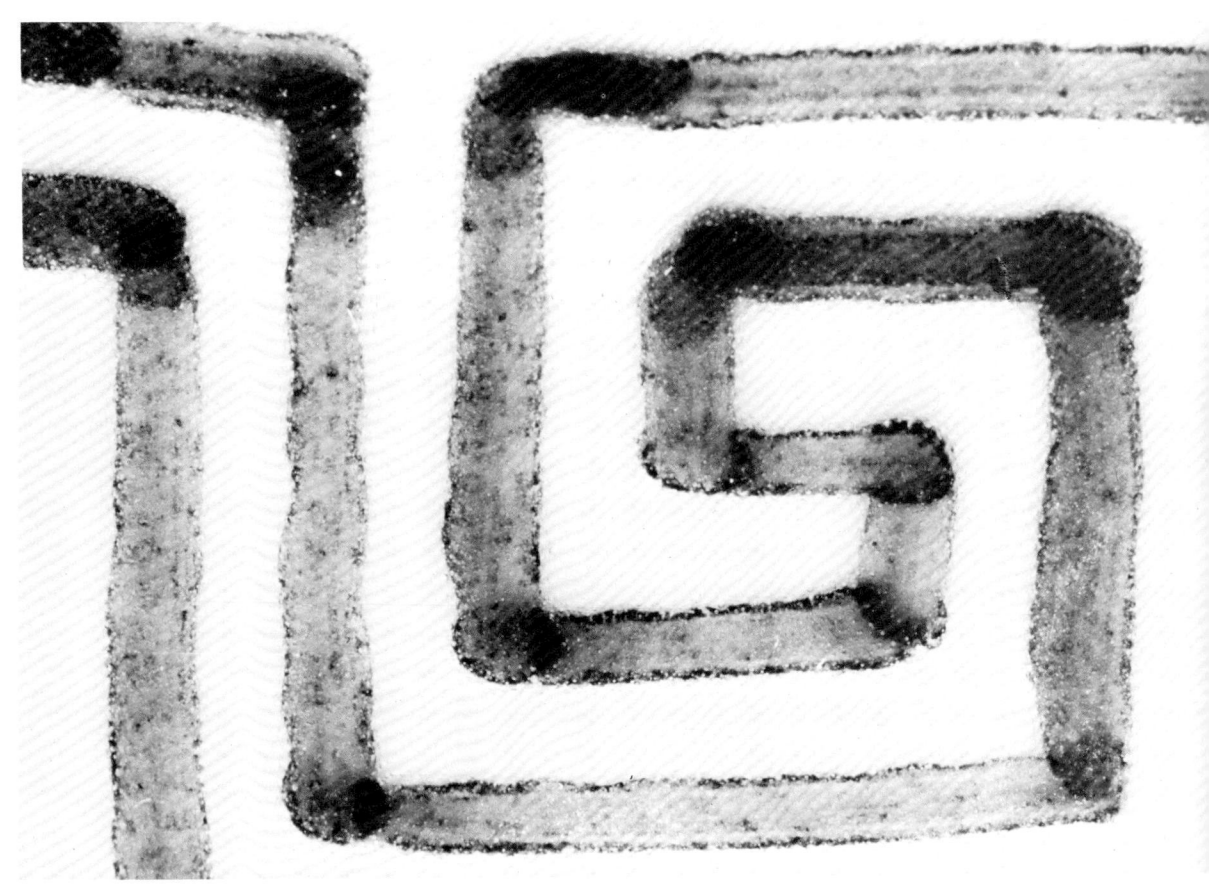

57   Detail. Key-fret pattern with *hollow lines.* Actual size of area: 5/16" H., ½" W.
From Kuang Hsu Blue and White Bowl in Plates 39-40, 50e, 52-56, 58-59.

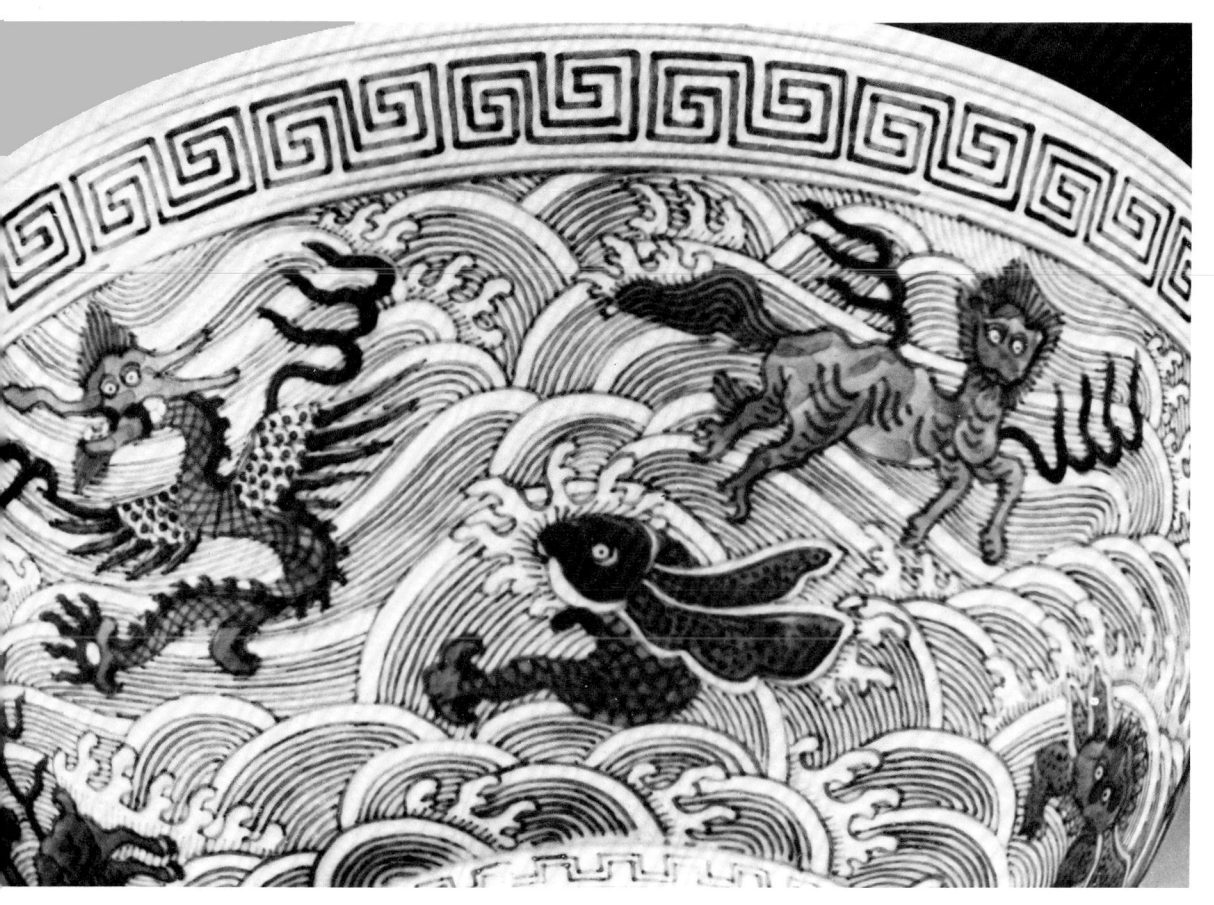

58 Detail. Winged Dragon and Mythological Animals over waves. From a distance all lines look solid. With the exception of long lines encircling bowl, every line is *hollow*. Kuang Hsu Blue and White Bowl in Plates 39-40, 50e, 52-57, 59.

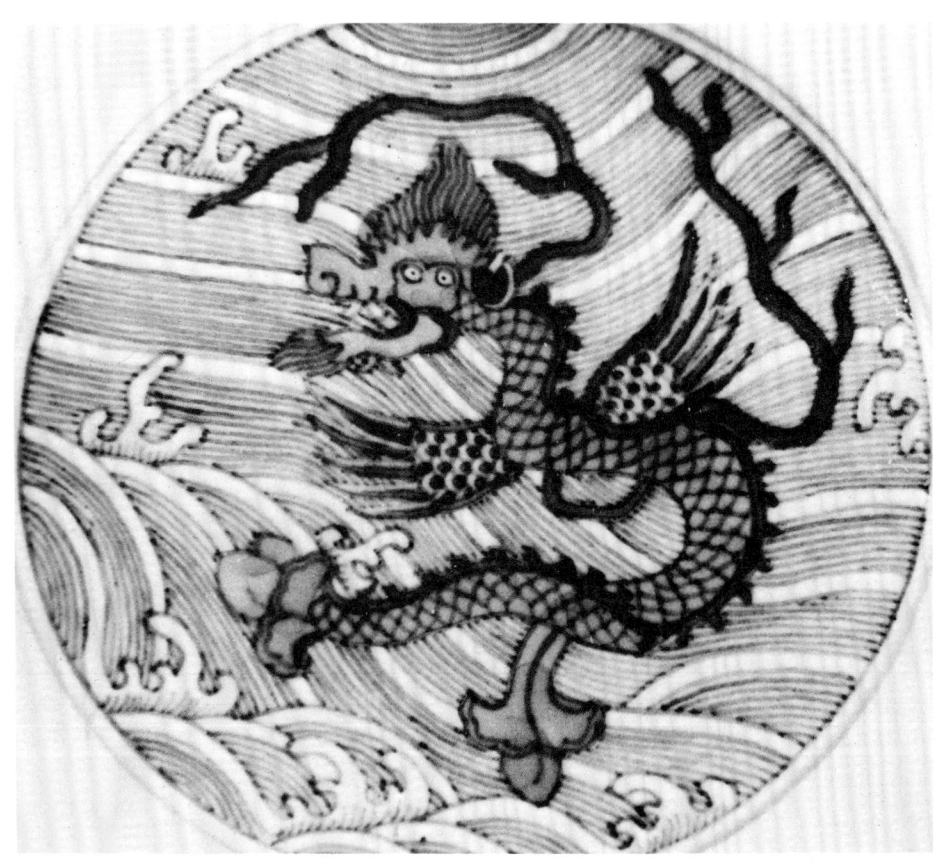

59 Detail. Interior of Kuang Hsu Bowl with the subject of "winged dragon, *fei yu.*" Medallion in well: 4" D. See Plates 39-40, 50e, 52-58. Collection of Wu Shu-Chen, San Francisco.

WINGED DRAGONS

The subjects of winged dragons and mythological animals on the bowl illustrated above are the same as the ones that decorate the well-known Ming Dynasty Ch'eng Hua stemcup recently sold at Sotheby Parke Bernet in London.[1] The above winged dragon, a nineteenth-century version, is different from the fifteenth-century one in details only. The main features of the two are the same; both are commonly called *fei yu. Fei yu* as well as two other types of winged dragons, the "foliated dragon" and *ying lung,* are seen in many porcelains. However, they are not uniformly identified. Sometimes, one winged dragon is confused for the other. (See Index under *fei yu* and *ying lung* for their respecitve Chinese characters).

Fei yu, literally "flying fish," is traced by Cammann to a 1459 statute regarding costume designs in the Ming Dynasty imperial court.[2] *Fei yu* is described as a dragon with "prominent bat form wings," a "forked caudal fin at the tip of its tail," and "fish's pectoral fins in place of forelegs but regular dragon's hindlegs." This type of dragon is not only used by "the designers of textiles but the decorators of porcelains."[3] Dragons with wings drawn with ventral fins in place of hindlegs and regular dragon's forelegs are also called *fei yu.*[4] In most cases, however, *fei yu* identifies the winged dragon without legs but having fins only (Plates 60 and 65).[5] Although all the above is called *fei yu,* it is usually translated as "mythical winged animals,"[6] "winged dragon with fish tail,"[7] "winged fish dragons,"[8] "flying fish-dragon,"[9] "flying dragon-fish,"[10] "flying dragon,"[11] and "dragon."[12] This type of dragon, when not identified as *fei yu,* is called *yun-lung* ("cloud dragon")[13] and in one text, inaccurately as *ying lung.*[14] In several cases, this winged dragon with fins, is even described differently each time when it appears in more than one illustration in one book.[15] *Fei yu* is also used generically to describe the "mythical animal" motif, that is, various animal creatures with wings depicted over a wave pattern.[16] The Chinese call this motif *hai shou* ("sea beasts")[17] or *jui shou* ("fabulous beasts").[18] *Fei yu* is usually seen with such "sea beasts" and a regular-looking fish with wings (Plate 58). Distinctly a separate subject of decoration, the dual combination of fish and dragon can be seen in some porcelains.[19] The carp transforming into a dragon is a symbol of a student's passing literary examinations.[20]

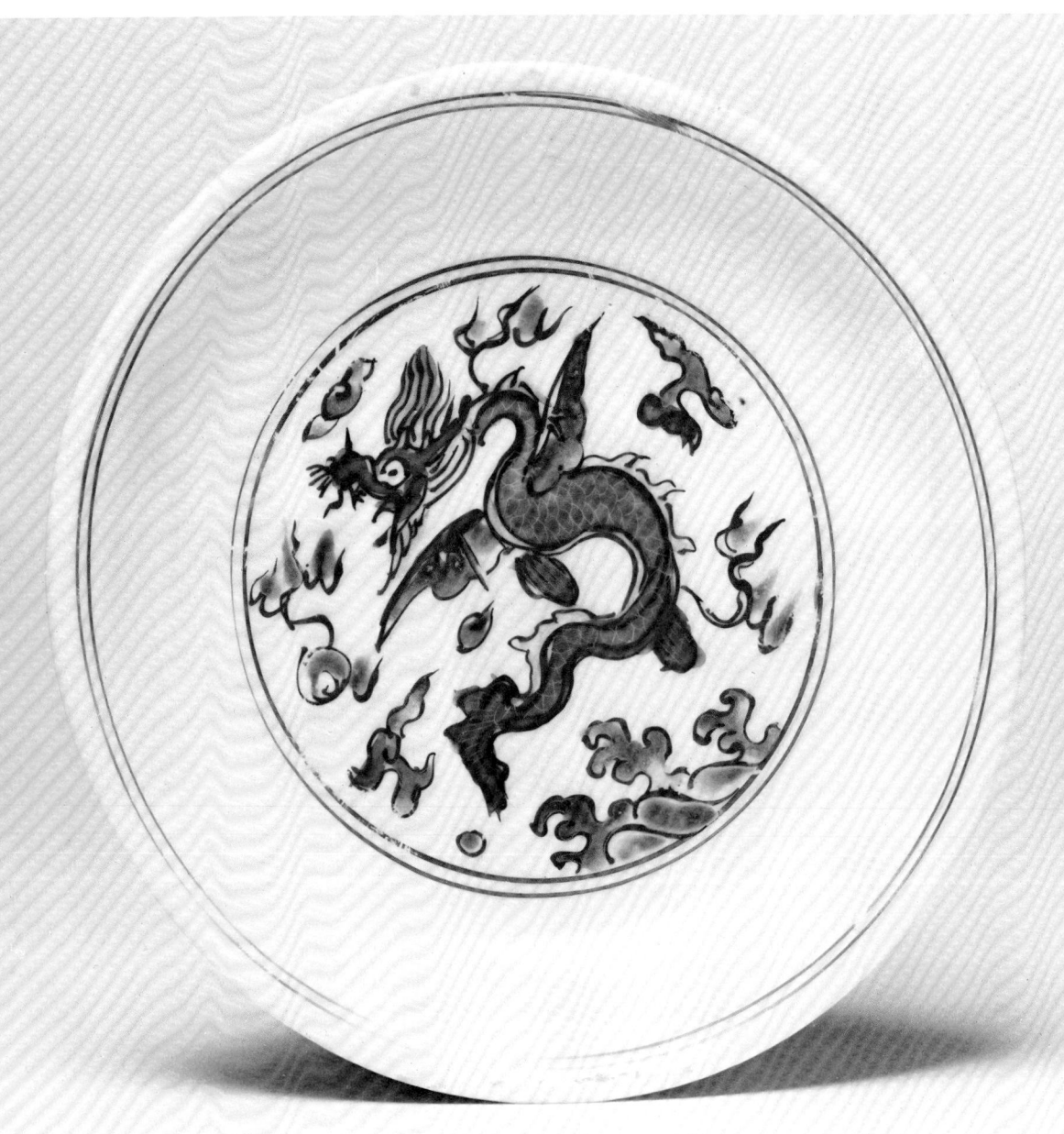

60 Plate, five-color overglaze enamels, with winged dragon commonly identified as *fei yu*. Ming Dynasty (16th Century). 1-5/16" H., 5¾" D. Collection of the Asian Art Museum of San Francisco, The Avery Brundage Collection, no. B67 P34.

One of the most interesting winged dragons is the one Pope describes with only two front legs and

> ... the rest of the body trails off in a succession of ornate scrolls. At the shoulders are small wings; the proboscidiform snout extends upward, and from the tip of the protruding tongue springs the stem of a lotus with leaves and a blossom. [21]

Pope describes this "beast" as a product of the latter half of the fifteenth century. Compared to other winged dragons, the scrolling body of this dragon is unique (Illustration 61).

The winged dragon with a scrolling body has been discussed under the name *"k'uei lung"* ("k'uei dragon").[22] *"K'uei"* is "an old name used in the Ch'ing Dynasty imperial court."[23] The features of this winged dragon called a "k'uei dragon" are listed as follows (quoted verbatim):

1. The upper lips of most of the dragons resemble elephants' trunks, protruding upward in a sweeping curve.
2. An Indian lotus blossom or strands of beads often spout from its mouth.
3. Usually only the two forelegs are shown, hind legs do not appear.
4. Most of the dragons have a pair of wings.
5. The rear portion of the body beginning from behind the forelegs is divided into foliage-like, curling patterns. [24]

The first appearance of the "k'uei dragon" is attributed to the early Ming Dynasty. Characteristics numbers 2 and 5 are stated to have first appeared in the Ch'eng Hua period (1465-87). Also referred to as *"hua shih lung"* ("flower-styled dragon"), it was a popular motif in export ware during the second half of the fifteenth century.[25]

Garner believes the "foliated dragon" "has a special significance, possibly Buddhist in origin" and contends that the innovation of this type of dragon takes place in the beginning of the early sixteenth century.[26] Addis describes the building of a Buddhist temple in Peking where a "foliated monster" design is observed with the inscription, "the first year of Ch'eng Hua" (1465).[27] The design combination of lotus, vajra (thunderbolt sceptre) and the "foliated

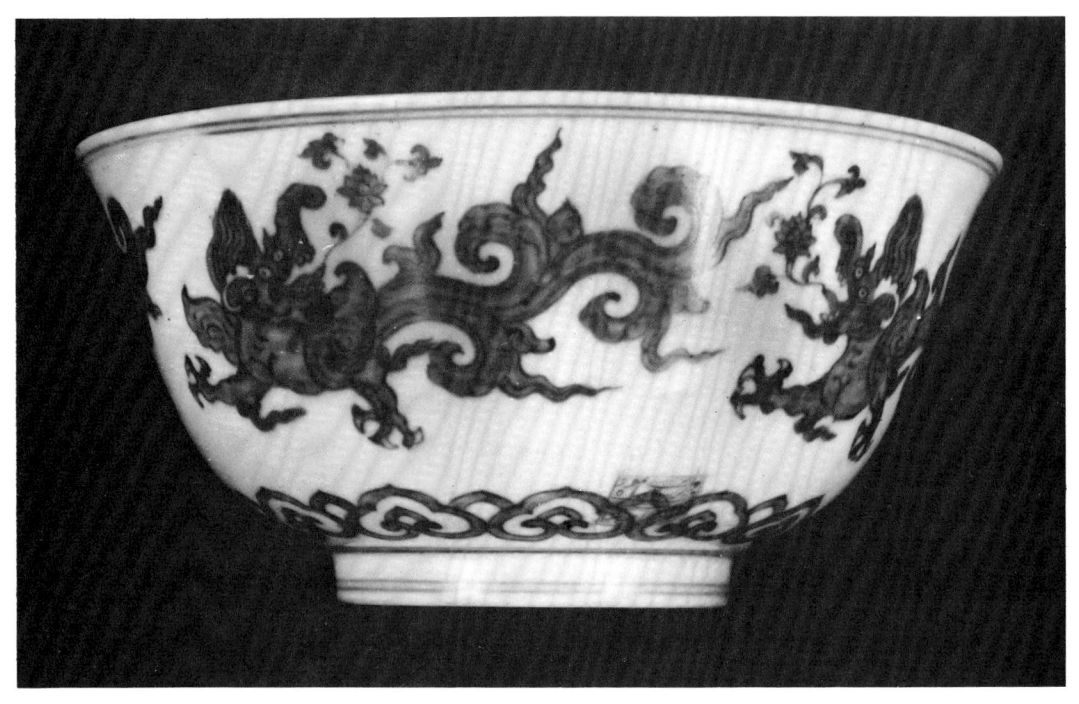

61 "Foliated Dragon," from Pope, *Chinese Porcelains From The Ardebil Shrine*, pl. 62. See Notes II, no. 25. Courtesy, John A. Pope.

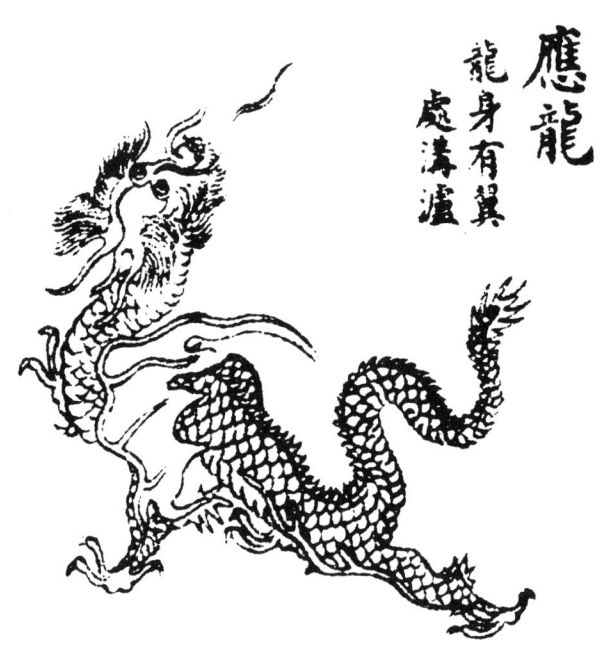

應龍
龍身有翼
處溝瀆

62 *Ying Lung* from the *Shan Hai Ching*.
See Notes II, no. 35.

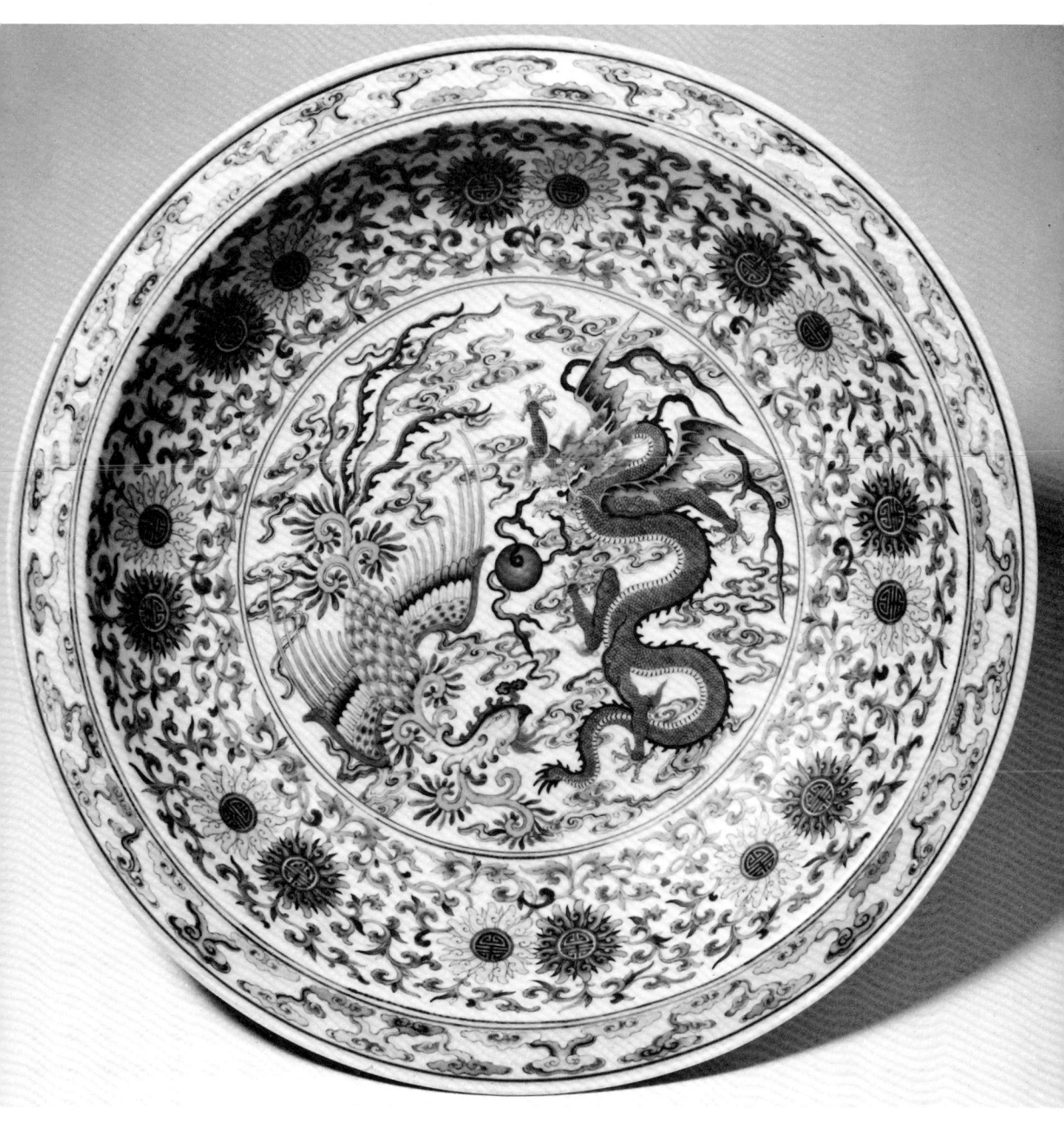

63   Platter, *tou ts'ai*, phoenix and *ying lung*. Yung Cheng mark and period (1723-35). See Plate 48 for reign mark on platter. 4" H., 17¾" D. Collection of the Asian Art Museum of San Francisco, The Avery Brundage Collection, no. B60 P269.

dragon" is observed in all the above descriptions.[28]   Even though Cammann does not discuss Buddhist influence or a "foliated dragon," he does observe that a late sixteenth-century lacquer box in the Low-Beer Collection shows a dragon with:

> . . . the body behind the wings dissolving into feathery wisps, giving the monster the appearance of a dragon-bird, and incidentally heightening its resemblence to a Hindu-Buddhist makara. [29]

A *"makara,"* also called a "water dragon," is a monster beast from Indian mythology and is a symbol of the "giver of the life-energy contained in the element water."[30] Interestingly, the term *fa lung* ("Buddhist-power dragon," or figuratively, "Buddhist dragon") has not been adopted for the "foliated dragon" that is seen with Buddhist motifs.[31]

The above writers seem to have overlooked a Chinese source of information for mythological animals, the *Shan Hai Ching (The Classic of the Universe).* [32] This book is devoted to geography and accounts for strange things in the animal and aquatic worlds. Dated as a pre-Han Dynasty book, the *Shan Hai Ching* is a record of a folklore period of China when there was still little distinction between fact and fiction. Subsequently, scholars of the T'ang and Sung Dynasties (618-1279 A.D.):

> . . . used the marvellous tales connected with these animals as a means of impressing the common people with the extraordinary quality of the Taoist doctrine, in the same way as the Buddhist propagandists gained a hearing through accounts of the miraculous powers of their deities. [33]

Although Chinese editions of this work are difficult to find, Schiffeler's recent English translation, entitled *The Legendary Creatures of the Shan Hai Ching,* makes it more easily obtainable.[34]

Illustration 62 is a *"ying lung"* from the 1917 edition of the *Shan Hai Ching.* It has a "dragon body, has wings, dwells in water courses."[35] This would seem to indicate the likelihood that the *ying lung* existed before the Ming Dynasty. Cammann states that in the Ming Dynasty the dragon, "provided with spreading wings, was then altered to *ying lung."*[36] *Ying lung,* a dragon with four legs, claws and wings, is sometimes seen in combination with the phoenix decorating porcelain. Although Cammann mentions that the *ying lung* "apparently did not survive into the Ch'ing Dynasty," a superbly drawn *ying lung* and phoenix can be seen in the Ch'ing Dynasty platter in the collection of the Asian Art Museum of San Francisco (Plate 63).[37]

Illustration 64 is a *"fei yu."* The description in *Shan Hai Ching* is:

> *Fei yu:* appearance of a suckling pig with red stripes; eating it, one would not be frightened by thunder and would be able to oppose soldiers; it appears in the waters of Cheng Hui. [38]

The appearance and description of this *fei yu* bears little resemblence to the winged dragon in porcelains that is identified as *fei yu* (Plates 60, 65).

Illustration 66 is a *"k'uei."* Under the section of "Wild Beasts" in the *Shan Hai Ching*, one can read:

> In the Liu Po Mountain that extends seven thousand lis into the Eastern Sea, there is a beast with the appearance of an ox, dark green body, no horn, one leg. Its movement in the waters always creates wind and rain; its glow is like the sun and moon; its sound, like thunder; its name, *k'uei.* [39]

No indication is made of this beast as being a type of dragon. However, the *K'ang Hsi Dictionary* explains that in the *Shuo Wen, k'uei* is a *"hsu,* an animal spirit that looks like a dragon with one leg." [40] In the *Shuo Wen* of the second century, the description of *k'uei* is: "A sacred spirit, *hsu;* looks like a dragon, one leg, **with** horn and human face."[41] In the *Tzu Yuan* of the eleventh century, the *k'uei lung* and *k'uei wen* are ancient bronze motifs. A *k'uei lung* and *k'uei feng* ("k'uei phoenix") are mentioned as names only.[42] The term, *"k'uei lung,"* is used by Laufer to identify the dragon "coiled in the form of a spiral" on old jade carvings. [43] This type of dragon has a tapir-like head and foliated body; wings and one leg can be found. A lotus flower protruding from the dragon's mouth is not part of this dragon design. Ancient bronzes with *k'uei lungs* can be observed in many fine examples of the Avery Brundage Collection in the Asian Art Museum of San Francisco.[44]

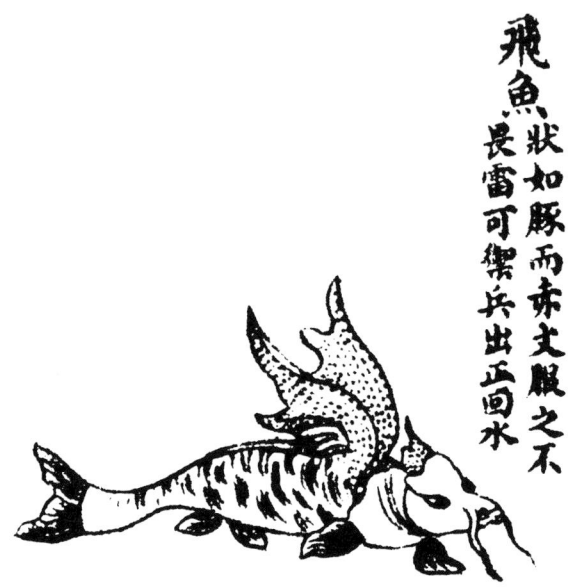

飛魚狀如豚而赤文服之不畏雷可禦兵出正回水

64 *Fei Yu* from the *Shan Hai Ching.*
See Notes II, no. 38.

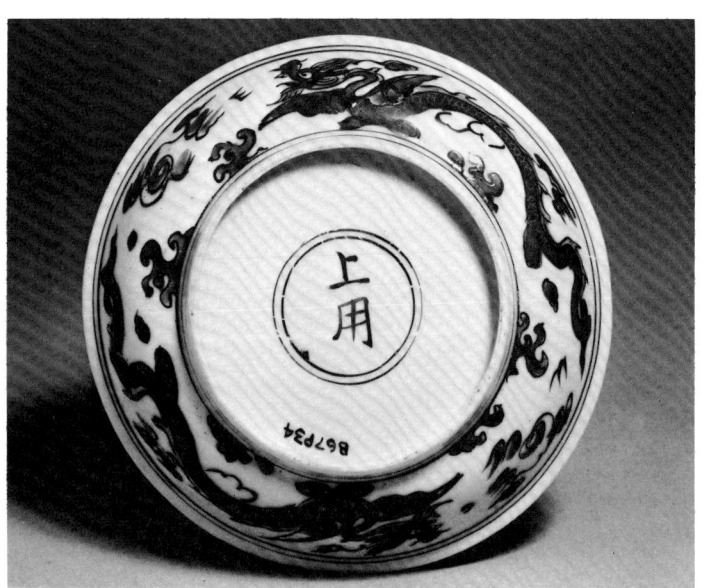

65 Back of Plate in illustration Plate 60, five-color over-glaze enamels, subject of winged dragons commonly identified as *fei yu.* See Notes II, no. 5. In center, "shang yung" ("for superior use." Medley in *Ming Poly-chrome Wares,* pl. VI, no. 761, translates "shang yung" as "for noble use"). Ming Dynasty (16th century). 1-5/16" H., 5¾" D. Collection of the Asian Art Museum of San Francisco, The Avery Brundage Collection, no. B67 P34.

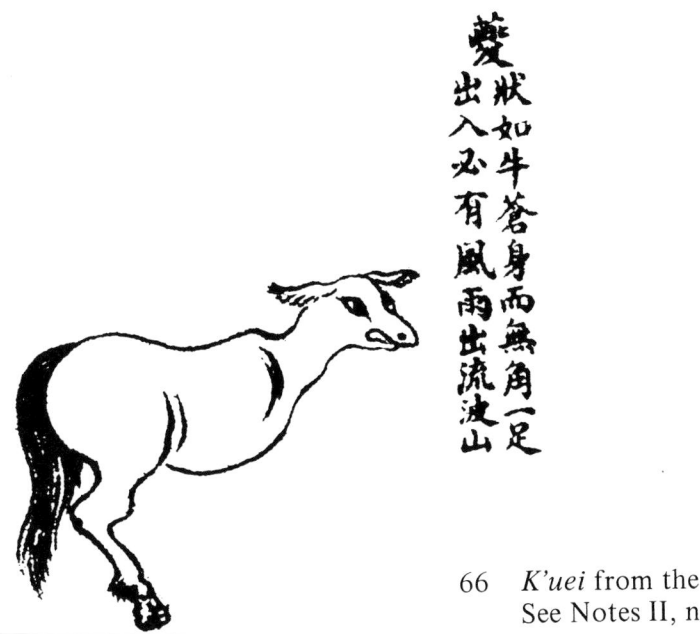

變狀如牛蒼身而無角一足
出入必有風雨出流波山

66   *K'uei* from the *Shan Hai Ching.*
      See Notes II, no. 39.

From the above information, it appears that only the *ying lung* has survived without change through the ages. *Ying lung* is a dragon with wings and having four legs with claws. What is presently called *"fei yu"* does not resemble *Shan Hai Ching's fei yu. Fei yu* is a winged dragon usually having all fins but not having more than one pair of legs (front or hind ones). The term *fa lung* (figuratively, "Buddhist dragon") appears to be more explicit than the term *k'uei lung* that is recently used to identify the "foliated dragon." The "foliated dragon" is the dragon with wings, two forelegs, a scrolling body and a lotus-flower complement. The vajra is often seen as a part of this decorative combination.

T'uan lung ("a coiled-up dragon"), a pattern name, is used to describe the "foliated dragon" with lotus flower in medallions decorating Ming Dynasty Ch'eng Hua *tou ts'ai* cups.[45] In this case, "Buddhist dragon medallions" may be more consistent with the above reasoning. Incised dragon medallions on Ch'ing Dynasty peach-bloom beehive-shaped waterpots are *t'uan lung* designs also. In order to distinguish this particular dragon from the others, perhaps this dragon design should be called "stylized *fei yu* medallions."[46] At last, all of them are dragons with wings. Or simply "winged dragons." Interestingly, a popular name for winged dragons in the vernacular Chinese is *fei lung* ("flying dragon").

CH'ING DYNASTY REIGN TITLES (SEAL SCRIPTS FROM PORCELAIN EXAMPLES)

Shun Chih

1644-1661

順治

Tao Kuang

1821-1850

道光

K'ang Hsi

1662-1722

康熙

Hsien Feng

1851-1861

咸豐

Yung Cheng

1723-1735

雍正

T'ung Chih

1862-1874

同治

Ch'ien Lung

1736-1795

乾隆

Kuang Hsu

1875-1908

光緒

Chia Ch'ing

1796-1820

嘉慶

Hsuan T'ung

1909-1912

宣統

NOTES I   THE HOLLOW LINE IN DATING CHINESE PORCELAINS

1. Chou, *Ch'ing Dynasty Porcelain.*

2. Young, *San Francisco Chronicle,* Bonanza Section, pp. 1-2, 12-13.

3. Bushell, *Chinese Art,* Vol. II, p. 43. Identical paragraph heading in Wilkinson, *Notes on Chinese Porcelain,* p. 13.

4. *Ibid.* Dismissing later Ch'ing porcelains with one sentence remark similar to this comment in Wilkinson, *op. cit.*

5. Hobson, *Chinese Pottery and Porcelain,* p. 263.

6. *Ibid.,* p. 267.

7. *Ibid.,* p. 271.

8. Hobson, *The Later Ceramic Wares of China,* p. 93.

9. Hobson, *Chinese Art,* p. 19.

10. Cox, *The Book of Pottery & Porcelain,* Vol. II, p. 605.

11. *Ibid.*

12. Jenyns, *Later Chinese Porcelain,* p. vii.

13. Chou, *Chinese Ceramics.*

14. Van Oort, *Chinese Porcelain of the 19th and 20th Centuries,* p. 14.

15. Medley, *The Chinese Potter,* p. 267.

16. *Ibid.*

17. Beurdeley, *A Connoisseur's Guide to Chinese Ceramics,* p. 275.

18. Van Oort, *op. cit.,* pp. 28-29.

19. Macintosh, *Chinese Blue & White Porcelain,* p. 143.

20. *Ch'ing Polychrome Porcelain,* p. xiv.

21. One of the Min Ch'iu Society members has now amassed many impressive later Ch'ing specimens that now make his ceramic collection a more comprehensive one. Of particular interest are his pieces with good quality Hsien Feng reign marks. Operating only three years, the Ching Te Chen kilns were destroyed by the T'ai P'ing Rebellion. Fine Hsien Feng porcelains with reign marks are not easy to find.

22. Chow and Drake, "Kuan-Yao and Min-Yao," *Archives of the Chinese Art Society of America,* pp. 54-74. See comment on Imperial and non-Imperial wares in Garner, *Oriental Blue and White,* pp. 7-8.

23. Wu Shu-chen is the President of the Chinese Calligraphy Society (San Francisco), a director of The Association of Chinese Calligraphers (New York), a Senior Member of the Chinese Art Appraisers Association, and a member of the American Society of Appraisers. Her fine collection of Chinese art is significantly rich in specimens of rare stone sculpture, bronzes, jade, paintings and ceramics from the Shang to the Ch'ing Dynasties. The greater part of this collection was inherited from her father, Dr. Wu Yueh, the late Chief Justice of a provincial Supreme Court in China, a famous jurist, scholar and collector. Admired as a calligraphy master, poet, painter, collector, and a keen appraiser of Chinese art, Wu Shu-chen has contributed immeasurably to making this publication possible.

24. Pope, *Chinese Porcelains From The Ardebil Shrine,* p. 84.

25. Medley, *op. cit.,* p. 214.

26. Hodgson, *How to Identify Old Chinese Porcelain,* p. 12.

27. Van Oort, *op. cit.,* p. 42.

28. *Ch'ing Polychrome Porcelain,* p. xiv.

29. Hodgson, *op. cit.,* p. 16.

30. Chait, "The Eight Prescribed Peachbloom Shapes Bearing K'ang Hsi Marks," *Oriental Art,* p. 131. See Valenstein, *A Handbook of Chinese Ceramics,* p. 201, pl. 138.

31. Garner, *op. cit.,* p. 71.

32. *Ibid.,* p. 53.

33. *The Arts of the Ming Dynasty*, p. 29.

34. Macintosh, *op. cit.,* p. 21.

35. *Ch'ing Polychrome Porcelain,* visible *hollow line* characteristic in
    a. p. 70, no. 108.
    b. p. 78, no. 126.
    c. p. 81, no. 132.

36. *Arts of the Celestial Empire* at I. Magnin, San Francisco, June, 1977.
    1-Week Exhibition and Sale of Chinese Porcelain Wares from the Reign of Ching Dynasty Emperor! at the Emporium in San Francisco Downtown and Stonestown, July 10-17, 1977.

    Similar incense burners with dated inscriptions in:
    a. *The Animal in Chinese Art,* pl. 3J, no. 83, dated 1786.
    b. Beurdeley, *op. cit.,* pl. 214, no. 116, dated 1624.
    c. *Chinese Blue and White Porcelain,* pl. 14d, no. 217, dated 1621.
    d. Garner, *op. cit.,* pp. 8, 35, 76, pl. 54, dated 1618.
    e. Jenyns, *op. cit.,*
       1) pl. VII, dated 1667.
       2) pl. XII, dated 1717.

37. Butterfield, Feb. 10, 1977, nos. 288, 294.

38. Blue and White plates with lotus design:
    a. *The Arts of the Ch'ing Dynasty,* no. 110, K'ang Hsi mark.
    b. *Chinese Blue and White Porcelain,* pl. 17f, no. 322, Kuang Hsu mark.
    c. Chou, *Chinese Ceramics,*
       1) p. 13, pl. 34 left, T'ung Chih mark, with additional overglaze turquoise enamel floral decoration.
       2) p. 13, pl. 34 right, Kuang Hsu mark.
    d. d'Argence, *A Decade of Collecting,* p. 71, pl. 79, Kuang Hsu mark.
    e. Garner, *op. cit.,* pl. 83B, Kuang Hsu mark.
    f. Roy Leventritt Collection, Asian Art Museum of San Francisco:
       1) no. 60 - 4 - 3, K'ang Hsi mark.
       2) no. 62 - 3, Tao Kuang mark.
    g. Macintosh, *op. cit.,* p. 87, pl. 65, Kuang Hsu mark.
    h. Osgood, *op. cit.,* pl. 62, row 2, right, "Yung Cheng."

    i.   Sotheby Parke Bernet Catalogue, Hong Kong,
            1) May 16, 1977, no. 106, K'ang Hsi mark.
            2) May 19, 1977, no. 511, Tao Kuang mark.

    j.   _____, London,
            1) Mar. 14, 1972, no. 162, Kuang Hsu mark.

    k. Van Oort, *op. cit.,*
            1) p. 42, pl. 45, T'ung Chih mark.
            2) p. 50, pl. 63, Kuang Hsu mark.
        An account of the production lists of the two periods are also given, pp. 39 - 41 on T'ung Chih wares and pp. 63 - 66 on Kuang Hsu ones.

39.   Butterfield, *op. cit.,* nos. 275, 280, 290, 300.

40.   Harris, "Art Experts," *Town & Country,* pp. 122-23. Comments are made by Henry Trubner on collecting Chinese and Japanese ceramics, also Mottahedehs on Chinese export porcelain, Max Loehr on Chinese bronzes and jades, and Laurence Sickman on Chinese painting and sculpture. See also Sotheby Parke Bernet's *Art at Auction,* 1976-77, p. 353, in which John Ayers comments on collecting Chinese works of art. See "Economy & Business," *Time,* August 8, 1977, p. 65. Robert Salomon Jr., of Salomon Brothers, the New York investment banking house, measured "the compound growth of nine assorted investments from 1968 to June 1977, a period in which the consumer price index increased at an annual rate of 6.2," and found that investment in Chinese ceramics was first, increasing at an annual rate of 23.2%, second was gold at 16%, old masters at 13%, coins at 12.3%, housing at 8.6% and stocks at 2.6%. See also Helen Harris, "A World of Chinese Ceramics," *Town & Country,* March, 1978, New York, pp. 144, 146-47. Also Joy Dewesse-Wehen, "West Coast Is Exciting Marketplace For Oriental Art," *Antique Monthly,* March, 1978, Tuscaloosa, Alabama, pp. 12-13C.

NOTES II   WINGED DRAGONS

1. Sotheby Parke Bernet Catalogue, London, July 5, 1977, no. 184. A Blue and White stemcup with iron red wave design, Ming Dynasty Ch'eng Hua, 4" H., 6 1/8"D.

    Kuang Hsu bowl with the same subject of decoration (Plates 52-59). Winged dragons and mythological animals can be seen in:

    a. *The Animal in Chinese Art,* pl. 5H, no. 164. A bowl with Ch'ien Lung mark. Design described as "fabulous beasts."

    b. *Blue-and-White Ware of the Ming Dynasty.*
        1) Vol. 2, pt. 2, p. 130, pls. 51 - 51b, Hsuan Te mark, *"hai shou."*
        2) Vol. 3, p. 42, pls. 11 - 11e, Ch'eng Hua mark, *"hai shou."*
        3) Vol. 4, p. 64, pls. 18 - 18e, Wan Li mark, *"hai shou."*

    c. *Ch'ing Porcelain from the Wah Kwong Collection,*
        1) No. 71, with "coral red" waves, Ch'ien Lung seal mark, *"jui shou."*
        2) No. 72, with "coral red" waves, Chia Ch'ing seal mark, *"jui shou."*

    d. Christie's Catalogue, New York,
        May 4, 1978, no. 281, Kuang Hsu mark, "winged dragon."

    e. Jenyns, *Ming Pottery and Porcelain,* p. 85, pl. 67, Ch'eng Hua mark, "fantastic sea monsters."

    f. Osgood, *Blue-and-White Chinese Porcelain,* pl. 41, "K'ang Hsi," design not described.

    g. *Oriental Works of Art,* PB 84, New York,
        Sale 604, Feb. 8, 1978, no. 319, Kuang Hsu mark, "dragon."

    h. Private collection, with "ch'ing hua chen p'in" mark in underglaze blue (see Index for Chinese characters), considered late 19th century.

    i. Sotheby Parke Bernet Catalogue, Los Angeles,
        Mar. 6, 1978, no. 1454, Chia Ch'ing seal mark, "fabulous animals."

    j. ——————, New York,
        Nov. 21, 1974, no. 302, Chia Ch'ing seal mark, "mythical beasts."

    k. Tsao, *Ming Dynasty Ch'eng Hua Porcelain,* nos. 94-96, *"hai shou."*

2. Cammann, "Some Strange Ming Beasts," *Oriental Art,* vol. 2, no. 3, 1956, pp. 95-96.

3. *Ibid.,* pp. 94, 96-97.
    Illustrations of *fei yu* with hindlegs only:

    a. *Ibid.,* p. 96, pl. 3, " 'flying fish' dragon."

    b. Macintosh, *Chinese Blue & White Porcelain,* p. 90, no. 67B, "sea dragons."

c. *Ming Blue-and-White,* p. 69, pl. 83, "dragons."

d. Sotheby Parke Bernet Catalogue, Hong Kong,
   Oct. 31, 1974, no. 98, "flying dragon, *fei yu,"*

4. Illustrations of *fei yu* with forelegs only:

   a. *Blue-and-White Ware of the Ming Dynasty,* vol. 1, p. 78, pls. 19-19c,
      "lung wen" and "dragon."

   b. Sotheby Parke Bernet Catalogue, London,
      Dec. 2, 1974, no. 523, "winged dragons."

   c. Tsao, *op. cit.,* no. 167, *"lung wen"* and "dragon."

5. Illustrations of *fei yu* with fins only:

   a. *The Animal in Chinese Art,* pl. 4B, no. 42, described as "flying fish
      dragon, *fei yu."*

   b. *The Arts of the Ming Dynasty,*
      1) pl. 45, no. 190, "mythical winged animals."
      2) pl. 45, no. 191, "mythical animals."

   c. Cammann, *op. cit.,* p. 96, pl. 2, " 'flying fish' dragon."

   d. *Catalogue of the 7th Annual Exhibition of Porcelain of Ch'ing Dynasty,*
      Min Ch'iu Society, Hong Kong, 1968, no. 46, "winged dragons."

   e. *Chinese Blue and White Porcelain,*
      1) pl. 10c, no. 116, "winged dragons."
      2) pl. 14d, no. 217, "winged dragons."

   f. *Chinese Ceramics From Japanese Collections,* no. 94, no. 50, "winged
      dragon, *ying lung."*

   g. d'Argence, *A Decade of Collecting,* p. 34, pl. 52, subject not described in
      detail. See Plates 60, 65.

   h. *Exhibition of Chinese Blue and White Porcelain,* p. 66, no. 24, *"fei lung"*
      and "sea dragons."

   i. Garner, *Oriental Blue and White,* p. 39, pl. 59A, design not described.

   j. Hobson, *The Wares of the Ming Dynasty,* p. 117, pl. 28, fig. 2, "dragon."

   k. Lee, *Asian Art,* p. 69, no. 54, "winged dragon."

   l. Medley, *Ming Polychrome Wares,* pl. VI, no. 761, "winged fish dragon."
      Similar to the one in the Asian Art Museum of San Francisco. See
      Plates 60, 65.

   m. _____, *Underglaze Blue and Copper Red,* pl. VI, no. A623, "winged
      fish dragons."

   n. *Sung - Ming,* p. 69, no. 86a, "dragon," See also footnote below, no. 15.
      c.

   o. Nguyet, *Arts of Asia,* cover, and p. 25, "flying dragon."

p. Sotheby Parke Bernet Catalogue, Hong Kong,
    1) Oct. 31, 1974, no. 67, "winged dragons with fish tails, *fei yu.*"
    2) Nov. 17, 1975, no. 194, "winged dragon, *fei yu.*"

q. _____, London,
    1) July 9, 1974, no. 205, "winged dragon with fish tail, *fei yu.*"
    2) July 30, 1974, no. 288, "winged dragon."
    3) July 5, 1977, no. 184, "winged dragon, *fei yu.*"
    4) Mar. 21, 1978, no. 197, "dragons," in a cloisonne enamel bowl.

r. _____, New York,
    1) Nov. 21, 1974, no. 382, "mythical beasts."
    2) Mar. 17, 1977, no. 244, "flying dragon *(fei yu)."*

s. Pope, *Chinese Porcelains From The Ardebil Shrine,* pl. 70, "winged dragons."

t. Valenstein, *A Handbook of Chinese Ceramics,* p. 157, pl. 99, *"fei yu,* flying fish dragons."

u. _____, *Ming Porcelain,* p. 68, no. 40, *"fei yu,* flying fish-dragon."

6. *The Arts of the Ming Dynasty,* p. 69, pl. 45, no. 190.

7. See above footnote no. 5. p. 1). and 5. q. 1).

8. See above 5. l.

9. See above 5. a.

10. Joseph, *Ming Porcelains,* p. 57, pl. 59.

11. a. *Exhibition of Chinese Blue and White Porcelain,* pp. 31, 66, no. 24, *"fei lung"* and "sea dragons."

    b. Sotheby Parke Bernet Catalogue, Hong Kong,
       Oct. 31, 1974, no. 98.

    c. _____, New York,
       Mar. 17, 1977, no. 244.

12. *Blue-and-White Ware of the Ming Dynasty,* vol. 1, p. 78, *"lung wen"* and "dragon."

13. *Chinese Blue & White Porcelain,* p. 29, no. 16.

14. *Chinese Ceramics From Japanese Collections,* p. 95, no. 50.

15. a. Macintosh, *op. cit.,*
      1) p. 36, no. 18, "fish dragons."
      2) p. 90, no. 67B, "sea dragons."
  b. Medley, *Underglaze Blue and Copper Red,*
      1) pl. II, no. 656, described on p. 25 as no. 655, "scaly fish dragons."
      2) pl. VI, no. A623, "winged fish dragons."
  c. *Sung - Ming,*
      1) p. 52, no. 49, "winged dragons."
      2) p. 54, no. 52, "winged fish dragons."
      3) p. 69, no. 86a, "dragon."

16. Beurdeley, *A Connoisseur's Guide to Chinese Ceramics,* p. 192.

17. See above footnotes, nos. 1. b. and 1. j.

18. a. See above no. 1. c.
  b. *Exhibition of Chinese Blue and White Porcelain,*
      1) p. 48, no. 88.
      2) p. 58, no. 127.

19. a. *The Animal in Chinese Art,* pl. 3E, no. 48.
  b. Frank, *Chinese Blue and White,* p. 80.
  c. Wirgin, "Ming Wares of the Lauritzen Collection," *Bulletin of the Museum of Far Eastern Antiquities,* no. 37, pl. 205, fig. 2, pl. 9, no. 14.
  d. Young, *Far Eastern Art in Upstate New York,* p. 53 no. 64.

20. a. Ball, *Decorative Motives of Oriental Art,* p. 6.
  b. Hayes, *The Chinese Dragon,* p. 19.
  c. Hobson, *Chinese Pottery and Porcelain,* II, p. 284.
  d. Williams, *Outlines of Chinese Symbolism & Art Motives,* p. 185.

21. Pope, *op. cit.,* p. 110.

22. Tsao, *op. cit.,* Chinese text, p. 7. English text, p. 12.

23. The Chinese text: " 清宮舊名 ." (p. 7)

    This is translated: "a term invented only much later by the Ch'ing imperial court to describe the design." (p. 12)

24. *Ibid.*

25. Illustrations of "foliated dragons" in:
  a. Addis, "Chinese Porcelains Found in the Philippines," *Transactions of the Oriental Ceramic Society,* vol. 37, pl. 48d. Described on p. 32 as a "winged monster with foliated tail and with a lotus issuing from its mouth. Probably of Cheng-te (1506-21)." Pl. 48c shows the well of this plate with a *fei yu;* this combination of "foliated dragon" and *fei yu* is not commonly seen.
  b. _____, *Some Buddhist Motifs As A Clue To Dating,* nos. 9-10. Instead of the lotus, three strings of beads issue from the dragon's mouth. Described as "foliated dragon."
  c. *The Animal in Chinese Art,*
    1) pl. 2J, no. 27, "ch'ih dragon."
    2) pl. 4A, no. 28, with cloud patterns and not lotus flower, *"ying-ch'ih."*
  d. *The Arts of the Ming Dynasty,*
    1) p. 69, pl. 46, no, 177, "dragon."
    2) p. 69, pl. 47, no. 186, "winged monster with elephant's trunk and phoenix tail, among clouds."
  e. *Blue-and-White Ware of the Ming Dynasty,* vol. 3, p. 32, pls. 6-6d, *"k'uei lung"* and "k'uei dragon."
  f. Christie's, Catalogue, London,
    Apr. 18, 1977, no. 109, "dragons."
  g. *Exhibition of Chinese Blue and White Porcelain,* no. 27, *"fei szu lung."* The body pattern is like bristles. See also Laufer, *Jade, A Study in Archaeology & Religion,* p. 170, fig. 78. Compare with the above examples listed in footnote above in b.
  h. Frank, *op. cit.,* p. 49, "dragon."
  i. Garner, *Chinese and Japanese Cloisonne Enamels,* pls. 31A, 32B, 33, "dragons . . . ."
  j. Joseph, *op. cit.,* p. 61, no. 66, with cloud pattern only, "fabulous animal . . . ." Compare with above c. 2).
  k. Lee, *Ming Blue-and-White,* no. 95, with lotus, "fabulous leonine creatures . . . ." Compare with above d.
  l. Low-Beer, "Chinese Lacquer of the Middle and Late Ming," *Bulletin of the Museum of Far Eastern Antiquities,* no 24, pl. 44, fig. 115, legs are not visible, "winged dragons."
  m. Macintosh, *op. cit.,* p. 106, no. 75, "foliated dragon."

n. Na Chih-liang, *The Emperor's Procession,* "foliated dragons" in flag insignia in paintings:
    1) p. 107, pl. 9, fig. 17.
    2) p. 119, pl. 17, fig. 5.
    3) p. 122, pl. 19, fig. 45.

o. Pope, *op. cit.,* pl. 62, "dragons with foliated tails."

p. Sotheby Parke Bernet Catalogue, London,
    Dec. 2, 1974, no. 293, "dragon . . . ."

q. _____, New York,
    Apr. 10, 1974, no. 28, "foliated monsters."

r. Tsao, *op. cit.,*
    1) nos. 44, 45, 72, 101, 102, 161, *"k'uei lung"* ("k'uei dragon").
    2) nos. 8, 49, *"t'uan lung."*

s. Waddell, *Tibetan Buddhism,* p. 500, with similar head features only, "thunder-dragons of the sky."

26. Garner, *op. cit.,* pp. 70-71, pl. 32B.

27. Addis, *Some Buddhist Motifs As A Clue To Dating,* pp. 3-5.

28. a. *Ibid.*
    b. Garner, *op. cit.,* p. 70.
    c. Pope, *op. cit.,* p. 110.
    d. Tsao, *op. cit.,* Chinese text, p. 8.

29. Cammann, *op. cit.,* p. 98.

30. Lauf, *Tibetan Sacred Art,* p. 12.
"Makara" is defined as a "crocodile, emblem of water" by Rowland in *The Art and Architecture of India,* p. 13.
"K'uei lung" associated with a "hippocamp" by Laufer, *op. cit.,* p. 222.

31. a. *The Animal in Chinese Art,* "Dragon," par. 5.
    b. Nott, *Chinese Culture in the Arts,* p. 25.
    c. A Chinese Buddhist concept of dragon is one that has a long snake body and not having any legs. See:

佛學大辭典台北啟明書局 , 1960, p. 443.

As "Fu dogs" (also called "Fo" or "Foo dogs," the lion-like figures at Buddhist temple entrances) are popular in the English vernacular language, the foliated dragon being called a "Fu dragon" would reflect a similar Buddhist relationship.

32. 山海經圖說, 上海會文堂, 新記書局印行.

33. Ferguson, *Chinese,* vol. VIII, p. 104.

34. Schiffeler, *The Legendary Creatures of the Shan Hai Ching.*

35. 山海經圖說, 卷五第一頁, 麟介.

36. Cammann, *op. cit.,* p. 95.

37. Illustrations of *ying lung* in:
    a. *Ibid.*
    b. Asian Art Museum of San Francisco, a Ch'ing Dynasty *tou ts'ai* platter, see Plate 63.
    c. Christie's Catalogue, London,
        Nov. 25, 1974, no. 238, "winged fish dragons."
    d. Sotheby Parke Bernet Catalogue, London,
        1) Nov. 27, 1973, no. 252, "scaly dragons."
        2) Nov. 27, 1973, no. 275, "winged dragons."
        —————, New York,
    e. 1) Jan. 24, 1975, no. 319, "winged dragon."

38. 山海經圖說, 卷五第三頁, 麟介.

    See Illustration 64. Compare with Plate 65. Description of Cheng Hui in Schiffeler, *op. cit.,* p. 119.

39. 山海經圖說, 卷十四, 大荒東經.

    See Illustration 66.
    山海經圖說, 卷三第五頁, 獸族.

40. 康熙字典, 丑集下攵部.

41. 說文解字, 又部.

42. 辭源, 丑集五零頁, 攵部.

    Also Hobson, *op. cit.,* pp. 292-93.

43. Laufer, *op. cit.,* pp. 188, 222, 225 - 227.

    Many such dragons are more like *fei yu.* See jade carving in the Asian Art Museum of San Francisco, no. B60 J400. Similar example in William Watson, *Style in The Arts of China,* Universe Books, New York, 1974, pl. 143.

44. a. d'Argence, *Bronze Vessels of Ancient China in the Avery Brundage Collection,* pp. 20, 22, 26, 32.

    b. *Osaka - San Francisco Exchange Exhibition,* 1970, p. 118.

    c. Trubner, *Asiatic Art,* p. 50, pl. 71, pp. 130-31.

45. a. Tsao, *op. cit.,* nos. 8, 29.

    b. *The Arts of the Ming Dynasty,* p. 69, pl. 46, no. 177, "dragon medallions."

46. Illustrations of incised dragon medallions on peachbloom beehive-shaped water-pots in:

    a. Ayers, *The Baur Collection,* vol. 3, pls. A313-16.

    b. Chait, "The Eight Prescribed Peachbloom Shapes Bearing K'ang Hsi Marks," *Oriental Art,* III, p. 135.

    c. d'Argence, *Avery Brundage Collection of Chinese Ceramics,* p. LXVc.

    d. Medley, *Ming and Ch'ing Monochrome,* cover and pl. IV, no. 580.

    e. Neave-Hill, *Chinese Ceramics,* p. 136, no. 156.

    f. Trubner, *op. cit.,* p. 194, no. 157.

Compare with coiled-dragons in:

    a. Laufer, *op. cit.,*

        1) p. 188, fig. 93.

        2) p. 225, fig. 129.

    b. Nott, *Chinese Jade,* p. 68, fig. 41, pl. L.

BIBLIOGRAPHY   English Texts

J. M. Addis, "Chinese Porcelain Found in the Philippines," *Transactions of the Oriental Ceramic Society,* vol. 37, London 1967-68.

_____, *Some Buddhist Motifs As A Clue To Dating,* Manila Trade Pottery Seminar, 1968.

The Animal in Chinese Art, Oriental Ceramic Society Exhibition Catalogue, London, 1968.

Art at Auction, 1973-74, Viking Press, New York, 1974.

The Arts of the Ch'ing Dynasty, Oriental Ceramic Society Exhibition Catalogue, London, 1964.

The Arts of the Ming Dynasty, Oriental Ceramic Society Exhibition Catalogue, London, 1957.

John Ayers, *The Baur Collection,* vol. 3, London, 1972.

_____, "The Malcolm Collection of Chinese Ceramics and Works of Art, " *Art at Auction,* 1976-77, Sotheby Parke Bernet, New York, 1977.

Katherine M. Ball, *Decorative Motives of Oriental Art,* Dodd, Mead & Co., New York, 1927.

Cecile and Michel Beurdeley, *A Connoisseur's Guide to Chinese Ceramics,* Harper & Row, New York, 1974.

Blue-and-White Ware of the Ming Dynasty, Porcelain of the National Palace Museum, Taipei, vols. 1 - 4, Cafa Co., Hong Kong, 1963.

A. D. Brankston, *Early Ming Wares of Chingtechen,* Vetch & Lee, Hong Kong, 1970.

Stephen W. Bushell, *Chinese Art,* London, 1904.

Butterfield & Butterfield Catalogue, Sale 2942, Feb. 10-11, 1977, San Francisco.

Schuyler Cammann, "Some Strange Ming Beasts," *Oriental Art,* vol. 2, no. 3, 1956.

Catalogue of the 7th Annual Exhibition of Porcelain of Ch'ing Dynasty, Min Ch'iu Society, Hong Kong, 1968.

Ralph Chait, "The Eight Prescribed Peachbloom Shapes Bearing K'ang Hsi Marks," *Oriental Art,* vol. 3, no. 4, 1957.

Chinese Blue and White Porcelain, Oriental Ceramic Society Exhibition Catalogue, London, 1954.

Chinese Ceramics From Japanese Collections, The Asia Society, New York, 1977.

Ch'ing Polychrome Porcelain, Hong Kong University and The Oriental Ceramic Society of Hong Kong, 1977.

Ch'ing Porcelain from the Wah Kwong Collection, Chinese University of Hong Kong, 1974.

Calvin Chou, *Chinese Ceramics,* Sing Tao Jih Pao Printing Dept., Hong Kong, 1960.

_____, *Ch'ing Dynasty Porcelain,* Berkeley, 1960.

E. T. Chow and F. S. Drake, "Kuan-Yao and Min-Yao," *Archives of the Chinese Art Society of America,* New York, 1959.

Christie's Catalogue, London,
   1) Nov. 25, 1974, no. 238.
   2) Apr. 18, 1977, no. 109.

_____, New York,
   1) May 4, 1978, no. 281.

Warren E. Cox, *The Book of Pottery & Porcelain,* Crown Publishers, New York, 1970.

Rene-Yvon Lefebvre d'Argence, *A Decade of Collecting,* Asian Art Museum of San Francisco, 1976.

_____, *Avery Brundage Collection of Chinese Ceramics,* Asian Art Museum of San Francisco, 1967.

_____, *Bronze Vessels of Ancient China in the Avery Brundage Collection,* Asian Art Museum of San Francisco, 1977.

Exhibition of Chinese Blue and White Porcelain, Oriental Ceramic Society of Hong Kong, 1975.

J. C. Ferguson, *Myth of All Races, Chinese,* vol. VIII, Cooper Square, New York, 1964.

Ann Frank, *Chinese Blue and White,* Walker & Co., New York, 1969.

Sir Harry Garner, *Oriental Blue and White,* Faber & Faber, London, 1954.

_____, *Chinese and Japanese Cloisonne Enamels,* Faber & Faber, London, 1970.

Leon Harris, "Art Experts," *Town & Country,* New York, December, 1977.

L. Newton Hayes, *The Chinese Dragon,* Shanghai, 1922.

R. L. Hobson, *Chinese Art,* London, 1927.

_____, *Chinese Pottery & Porcelain,* London, 1915.

_____, *The Later Ceramic Wares of China,* London, 1925.

_____, *The Wares of the Ming Dynasty,* London, 1923.

Willoughby Hodgson, *How to Identify Old Chinese Porcelain,* Methuen, London, 1908.

Soame Jenyns, *Later Chinese Porcelain,* Faber & Faber, London, 1925.

_____, *Ming Pottery & Porcelain,* Faber & Faber, London, 1953.

A. M. Joseph, *Ming Porcelains,* Bibelot, London, 1971.

D. I. Lauf, *Tibetan Sacred Art,* Berkeley, 1976.

Berthold Laufer, *Jade, A Study in Chinese Archaeology & Religion,* Dover, New York, 1974.

Jean Gordon Lee, *Ming Blue-and-White,* Philadelphia Museum Bulletin, 1949.

Sherman Lee, *Asian Art,* Asia House, New York, 1970.

_____, *Far Eastern Art,* Prentice Hall, New Jersey, 1973.

Fritz Low-Beer, "Chinese Lacquer of the Middle and Late Ming Period," *Bulletin of the Museum of Far Eastern Antiquities,* no. 24, 1952.

Duncan Macintosh, *Chinese Blue & White Porcelain,* Charles E. Tuttle, Vermont, 1977.

Margaret Medley, *The Chinese Potter,* Charles Scribner's Sons, New York, 1976.

_____, *Ming & Ch'ing Monochrome,* London, 1973. See comments on this work by Clarence F. Shangraw under "Bibliographia" of *Artibus Asiae,* XXXIX, 2, 1977, pp. 156-59.

_____, *Ming Polychrome Wares,* London, 1966.

_____, *Underglaze Blue & Cooper Red,* London, 1976.

Ming Blue-and-White, Museum of Far Eastern Antiquities Exhibition Catalogue, no. 1, 1964.

Monochrome Ceramics of Ming & Ch'ing Dynasties, Hong Kong Museum of Art, Hong Kong, 1977.

Hugo Munsterberg, *Dragons in Chinese Art,* China Institute in America, New York, 1972.

Na Chih-liang, *The Emperor's Procession,* Taiwan, 1970.

W. B. R. Neave-Hill, *Chinese Ceramics,* St. Martin's Press, New York, 1975.

Tuyet Nguyet, "Ken Baas, Explorer Collector," *Arts of Asia,* Hong Kong, May-June, 1973.

Stanley C. Nott, *Chinese Culture in the Arts,* New York, 1946.

_____, *Chinese Jade,* Charles Scribner's Sons, New York, 1937.

Oriental Works of Art, PB 84, New York, Catalogue 604, Feb. 8, 1978, no. 319.

Osaka – San Francisco Exchange Exhibition, San Francisco, 1970.

Cornelius Osgood, *Blue-and-White Chinese Porcelain,* Ronald Press, New York, 1956.

John A. Pope, *Chinese Porcelains From the Ardebil Shrine,* Smithsonian Institution, Washington, D. C., 1956.

Benjamin Rowland, *The Art and Architecture of India,* Penguin Books, New York, 1977.

John W. Schiffeler, *The Legendary Creatures of the Shan Hai Ching,* Oriental Cultural Service, Taipei, 1977.

Sotheby Parke Bernet Catalogue, Hong Kong,
    1) Oct. 31, 1974, nos. 67, 98.
    2) Nov. 17, 1975, no. 194.
    3) May 16, 1977, no. 106.
    4) May 19, 1977, nos. 511, 519.
    _____, London,
    1) Mar. 14, 1972, no. 162.
    2) Nov. 27, 1973, nos. 252, 275.
    3) Jul. 9, 1974, no. 205.
    4) Jul. 30, 1974, no. 288.
    5) Dec. 2, 1974, nos. 293, 523.
    6) Jul. 5, 1977, no. 184.
    7) Mar. 21, 1978, no. 197.
    _____, Los Angeles,
    1) Mar. 6, 1978, no. 1454.
    _____, New York,
    1) Apr. 10, 1974, no. 28.
    2) Nov. 21, 1974, nos. 302, 382.
    3) Jan 24, 1975, no. 319.
    4) Sept. 23, 1976, no. 338.
    5) Mar. 17, 1977, no. 244.

Sung - Ming, Treasures from the Holger Lauritzen Collection, Museum of Far Eastern Antiquities Exhibition Catalogue, no. 3, 1965.

Henry Trubner, *Asiatic Art,* Seattle Art Museum, 1973.

Teresa Tsao, *Ming Ch'eng Hua Porcelain,* Taipei, 1976.

Suzanne G. Valenstein, *A Handbook of Chinese Ceramics,* Metropolitan Museum of Art, New York, 1975.

_____, *Ming Porcelain,* China Institute in America, New York, 1971.

H. A. Van Oort, *Chinese Porcelain of the 19th & 20th Centuries,* Lochem, 1977.

L. A. Waddell, *Tibetan Buddhism,* Dover, New York, 1972.

F. E. Wilkinson, *Notes on Chinese Porcelain,* Shanghai, 1908.

C. A. S. Williams, *Outlines of Chinese Symbolism & Art Motives,* Dover, New York, 1976.

Jan Wirgin, "Ming Wares of the Lauritzen Collection," *Bulletin of the Museum of Far Eastern Antiquities,* no. 37, 1965.

Martie W. Young, *Far Eastern Art in Upstate New York,* Cornell University, New York, 1976.

Nes Young, "Tudor Setting for Ancient Art," *San Francisco Chronicle,* Bonanza Section, Sept. 25, 1960.

accumulations in hollow lines
26 - 27.
Fig. 7, 10.
Pls. 15, 38, 52, 54 - 57.

Buddhist dragon
See *fa lung,* "foliated
dragon."
80.
II, 28, 31.

Ch'eng Hua   成化
(1465 - 87)

Cheng Te   正德
(1506 - 21)

Chia Ching   嘉靖
(1522 - 66)

Chia Ch'ing   嘉慶
(1796 - 1820)

chi chao tsun   雞罩罇
23.

Ch'ien Lung   乾隆
(1736 - 95)

ch'ing hua chen p'in   珍清
"elegant and   品華
magnificent
treasures."
I, 1. h.

ch'ih lung   螭龍
II, 25. c.

Ch'ing Dynasty   清朝
(1644 - 1912)

Great Ch'ing   大清

collecting trends
31.
I, 40.

cracked line   龜裂線
Fig. 12.
Pl. 51.

dated inscription on incense
burners
30.
I, 36.
Pl. 13.

dot in *hollow line*   淡心線之
27.   濃聚點
Fig. 8.
Pls. 15, 28, 54 - 55.

dragon medallions   圍龍
See *t'uan lung.*
II, 45 - 46.

fa lung   法龍
80.
II, 31.

fei lung   飛龍
II, 5. h., 11. a.

fei szu lung   飛絲龍
II, 25. g.

fei yu 飛魚
  75.
  II, 3 - 5, 38, 43.
  Pls. 58 - 60, 64 - 65.

"foliated dragon"
  See *fa lung.*
  77.
  II, 25.
  Fig. 61.

grouping porcelains for study
  29.

hai shou 海獸
  II, 1. b., 1. j.

hollow line 淡心線
  See *tan shin hsien*
  17.
  Fig. 3.
  Pls. 16 - 18, 20 - 21, 24, 26 -
    29, 52, 54 - 57.

hollow line character
  I, 35.
  Fig. 4.
  Pls. 35 - 36, 39, 45 - 46, 50.

hollow line reign mark
  I, 35.
  Pls. 15, 38, 40, 43, 47,
    49.

hollow line type
  Pls. 31, 38 - 40.

Hsien Feng 咸豐
  (1851 - 61)

hsu 81. 魖

Hsuan Te 宣德
  (1426 - 35)

Hsuan T'ung 宣統
  (1909 - 12)
  Pl. 15.

hua shih lung 花式龍
  "flower-styled dragon."
  See *fa lung.*

jui shou 瑞獸
  II, 1. c.

K'ang Hsi 康熙
  (1662 - 1722)

K'ang Hsi Dictionary 康熙字典
  II, 40.

Kuang Hsu 光緒
  (1875 - 1908)

kuan yao 官窰
  16.
  I, 22.

kuei mao 癸卯
  Pl. 13.

k'uei 夔
  77.
  II, 39.
  Fig. 61.
  Pl. 65.

k'uei feng 夔鳳
  "k'uei phoenix."

k'uei lung 夔龍
  II, 25. r., 30.

k'uei wen   81.   蘷紋

lotus design, Blue and
    White dishes
    31.
    I, 38.

lung   龍
    "dragon."

lung wen   龍紋
    II, 4. a.,
        4. c., 12.

makara
    80.
    II, 30.

market trends
    30.
    I, 40.

min yao   民窰
    16.
    I, 22.

monochrome porcelain
    See peachbloom

mythological animals
    See *Shan Hai Ching*
    75.
    II, 1.
    Pls. 53, 58.

nien chih   年製
    "year made."
    "made in the
        reign of . . ."

peachbloom beehive-shaped
    waterpots
    See *chi chao tsun,*
        t'ai po tsun.
    23.
    I, 30.
    II, 46.

pinholes in glaze
    29.
    Pls. 14 - 15, 49, 50a.

reign marks   20.
    See "Ch'ing Dynasty Reign
        Titles."

ring in *hollow line*   淡心線之
    27.   圓圈點
    Fig. 9.
    Pls. 27 - 28, 55.

Shan Hai Ching   山海經
The Mountain and Sea Classic,
or *The Classic of the Universe.*
II, 32.

Shun Chih   順治
(1644 - 61)

Shuo Wen   說文
    II, 41.   (說文解字).

solid line   密心線
    Fig. 1.
    Pl. 33.

solid line character
    Fig. 2.
    Pls. 37, 41 - 42, 48.

split line   分間線
    29.
    Fig 11.
    Pl. 46.

t'ai po tsun   太白罇
    23.

Tai Tung k'ou ching 岱東叩敬
    Pl. 13.

tan hsin hsien   淡心線
    "pale heart line."

Tao Kuang   道光
    (1821 - 50)

tou ts'ai   鬭彩

t'uan lung   團龍
    "coiled dragon (design)."
    dragon medallions.
    83.
    II, 25. r., 45 - 46.

T'ung Chih   同治
    (1864 - 74)

twentieth–century wares
    23.

Tzu Yuan   辭源
    II, 42.

Wan Li   萬曆
    (1573 - 1619)

Winged Dragons
    See *fa lung, fei yu,*
        "foliated dragon" and
        ying lung.
    75 - 83.
    II, 1.
    Pls. 58 - 63.

ying-ch'ih   應螭
    II, 25. c.

ying lung   應龍
    80.
    II, 5. f., 35, 37.
    Pls. 62 - 63.

Yung Cheng   雍正
    (1723 - 35)

yun lung   75.   雲龍

SPONSORS' INDEX

APPRAISERS COMPANY OF SAN FRANCISCO
ARTIBUS ASIAE
CHINESE ART APPRAISERS ASSOCIATION
CHINESE CALLIGRAPHY SOCIETY
CHOU CH'IN HAN & ASSOCIATES
DAIBUTSU
G. T. MARSH AND COMPANY
G. L. MORRIS
ORIENTAL ART
ORIENTAL PORCELAIN GALLERY
SAN FRANCISCO BAY ANTIQUE SHOWS
STEWARD'S TREASURE HOUSE

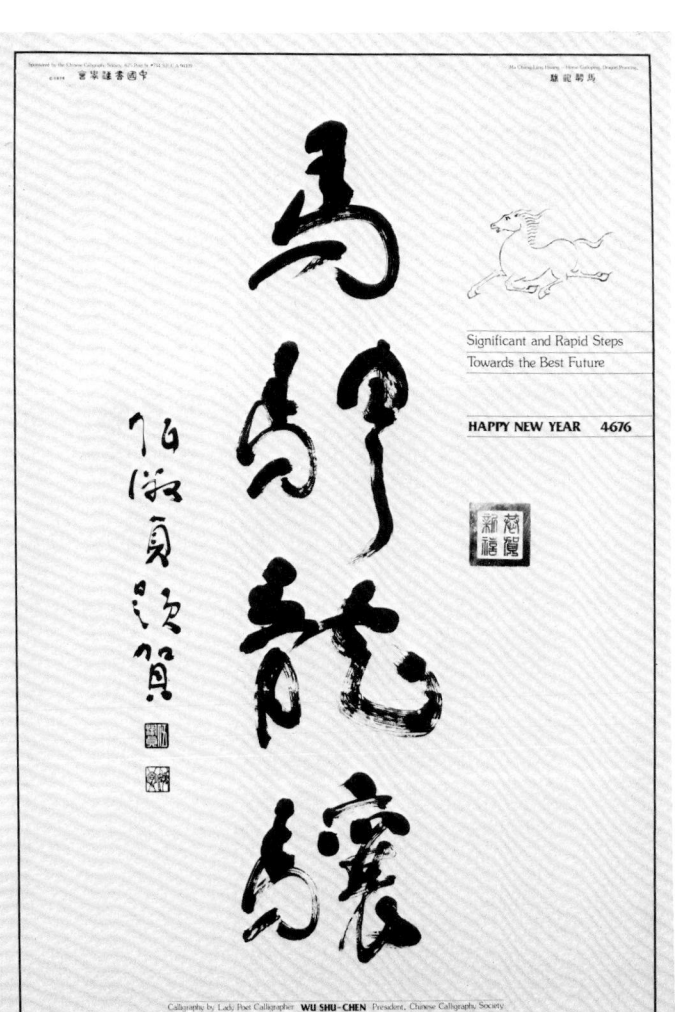

Calligraphy Poster, sponsored by the Chinese Calligraphy Society, 1978. Composition and calligraphy by Wu Shu-Chen, the President of the Society. Ink on Chinese-red paper, gold stamped, 17" x 24." $7.00 each. Available from the Society, and also from the museums:

University Art Museum Bookstore
2626 Bancroft Way
Berkeley, California 94920

Oakland Museum Bookstore
1000 Oak Street
Oakland, California 94607

會學漢書國中

CHINESE CALLIGRAPHY SOCIETY

625 POST STREET
SAN FRANCISCO, CALIFORNIA 94109

The Chinese Calligraphy Society is a non-profit organization devoted to promoting the appreciation and preservation of the literary and traditional art of Chinese calligraphy.

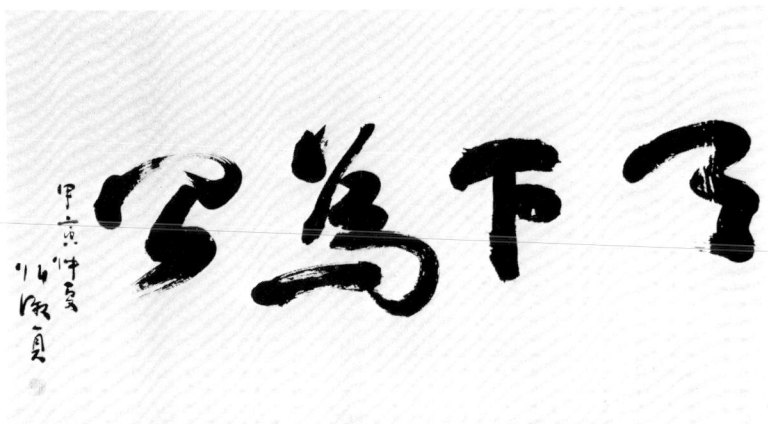

"Equality Under Heaven," quotation from *Book of Rites* by Confucius, calligraphy by Wu Shu-Chen, 1975. Ink on yellow, sprinkled gold, antique paper, 27" x 51." Courtesy, Museum of the Chinese Historical Society of America, San Francisco.

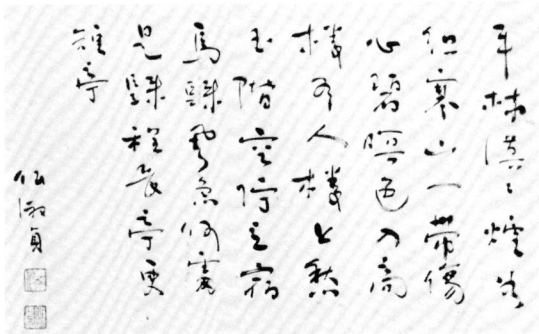

Poem by Li Po of the T'ang Dynasty, deep sentiments of being home sick and lonely. Calligraphy by Wu Shu-Chen, President of the Chinese Calligraphy Society. Ink on silk, 33" x 19." In the Exhibition sponsored by The Association of Chinese Calligraphers of America (New York, 1977) and in the Exhibition sponsored by the Chinese Library of America (San Francisco, 1978).

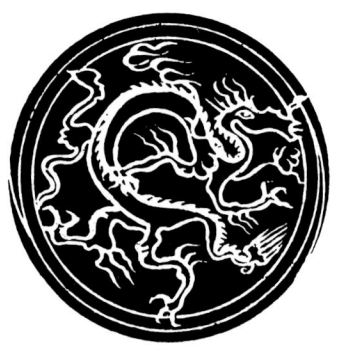

ARTIBUS ASIAE

INSTITUTE OF FINE ARTS · NEW YORK UNIVERSITY

Quarterly of Asian Art and Archæology for Scholars and Connoisseurs

Near — East India and Southeast Asia — Far East — The Migrations

Editorial Board:

Alexander C. Soper. *Editor-in-chief*

Richard Ettinghausen — Alexander B. Griswold — Stella Kramrisch — Edith Porada

**ILLUSTRATIONS OF PREVIOUSLY UNPUBLISHED ART OBJECTS AND DOCUMENTS
RECENT DISCOVERIES · NEW STUDIES OF OTHER MATERIAL · BOOK REVIEWS**

Volume XL (1978)

Artibus Asiae, a quarterly publication devoted to Asian art and archaeology, was started in 1925 and has continued regularly since, with the exception of the war years. Rather than attempting to repeat or to popularize material that is already available to scholars, it aims to present new discoveries, previously unpublished objects of art, and all sorts of new studies. Each issue contains detailed book reviews. It is consequently useful not only to research scholars, but also to collectors and connoisseurs who wish to familiarize themselves with the authentication, associations, and dating of the Asian antiquities that interest them. It is naturally indispensable to libraries, universities, museums, and institutions engaged in any branch of Asian studies. In addition, it maintains a standard of print and illustration that makes each issue an object of beauty in its own right.

The Journal is indispensable to all Connoisseurs,
Libraries, Museums, philological Seminaries, and all Institutions devoted to Asiatic research
World-wide circulation

Subscription price: U.S. $ 38.– or Swiss Francs 75.– per year (plus postage)
Each volume (4 issues) about 350 pages quarto, richly illustrated

---

ARTIBUS ASIAE SUPPLEMENTA
A series of full-length books dealing with kindred subjects
So far Supplements Nos. I–XXXIV have been published

		Swiss frs. or US. $	
XXIV	A. C. Soper: *Textual Evidence for the Secular Arts of China in the Period from Liu Sung through Sui (A. D. 420–618)*, Excluding Treatises on Painting	30.—	15.—
XXV	Gordon H. Luce: *Old Burma—Early Pagán.* 3 vols.		120.—
XXVI	J. M. Nanavati and M. A. Dhaky: *The Maitraka and the Saindhava Temples of Gujarat*	50.—	25.—
XXVII	Richard Barnhart: *Marriage of the Lord of the River. A Lost Landscape by Tung Yüan*	60.—	30.—
XXVIII	Stanley J. O'Connor: *Hindu Gods of Peninsular Siam*	48.—	24.—
XXIX	Charles Archaimbault: *La Course de Pirogues au Laos.* Un complexe culturel	70.—	35.—
XXX	Chu-tsing Li: *A Thousand Peaks and Myriad Ravines.* Chinese Paintings in the Charles A. Drenowatz Collection. 2 vols.	156.—	78.—
XXXI	Kiyohiko Munakata: *Ching Hao's PI-FA-CHI: A Note on the Art of Brush*	32.—	16.—
XXXII	Milo Cleveland Beach: *Rajput Painting at Bundi and Kota*	76.—	38.—
XXXIII	John C. Huntington: *The PHUR-PA, Tibetan Ritual Daggers*	76.—	38.—
XXXIV	Anne De Coursey Clapp: *WEN CHENG-MING: The Ming Artist and Antiquity*	76.—	38.—

Orders and Subscriptions are accepted through any agent or bookseller, or directly by

ARTIBUS ASIAE – PUBLISHERS · 6612 ASCONA · SWITZERLAND

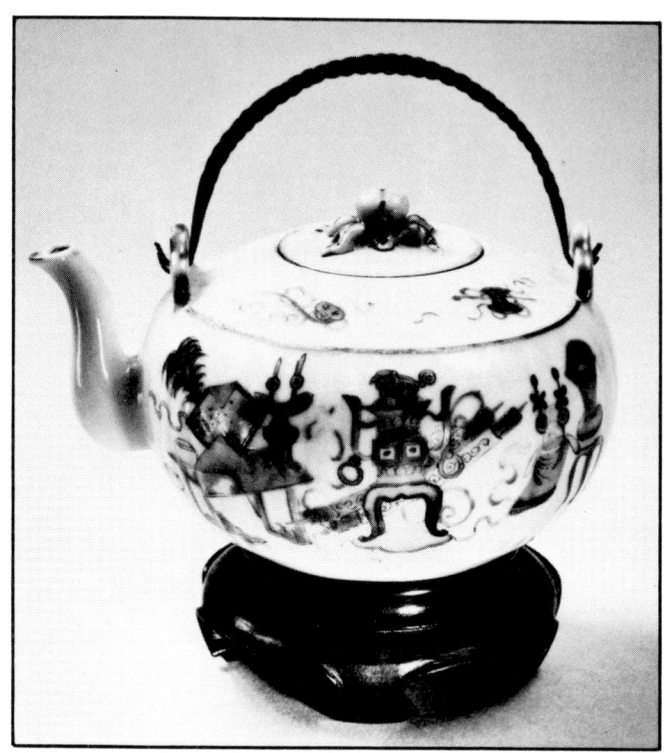
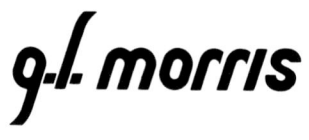

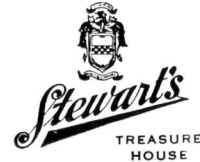

DAIBUTSU

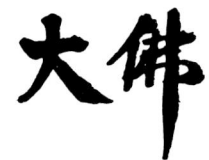

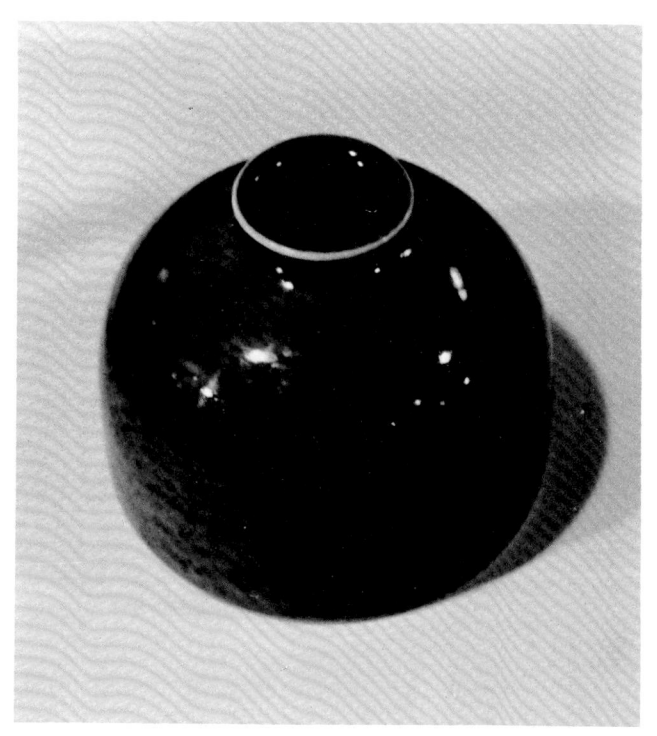

Chinese and Japanese Arts

3028 FILLMORE STREET
SAN FRANCISCO, CALIFORNIA 94123
JOrdan 7-1530

G. T. Marsh & Co.

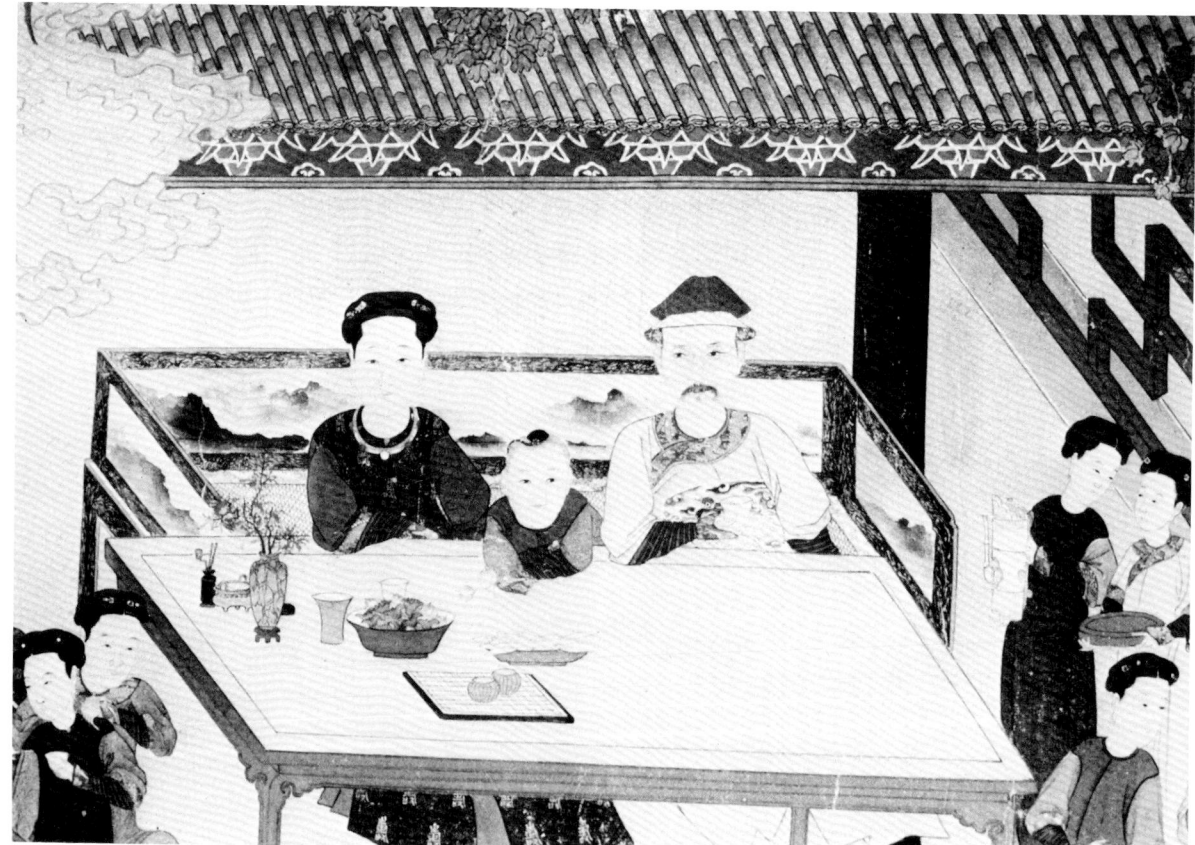

Detail from an unusually large Chinese genre painting of a mandarin and his family at leisure. The crane emblem on the man's garment signifies the highest rank in the civil service. Ink and color on silk. Painting only: 9 feet, 2 inches (2.8 M) in height. Width is 7 feet, 10 inches (2.4 m). Above detail: 12 x 18 inches (30.5 x 46 cm).

Signed: Lui Hsiang K'ai (劉祥開).
Dated: Second year of Shun Chih (1645).
Provenance: Marsh Family Purchase, Peking, China, 1922.
        Recently brought up from basement storage rooms.
        Painting No. 20812.